A GUIDE TO THE BOOK

TEF Study Guides

This series of textbooks is sponsored and subsidized by the Theological Education Fund in response to requests from theological teachers and students in Africa, Asia, the Caribbean, and the Pacific. Attention is given to problems of interpretation and application arising in those areas as well as in Europe and America, and to the particular needs of readers using English as a second language.

ALREADY PUBLISHED

1. A Guide to the Parables
2. A Guide to St Mark's Gospel
3. A Guide to the Book of Genesis

IN PREPARATION

Old Testament: History–Introduction–Theology
A Guide to Exodus
A Guide to Twenty Psalms
A Guide to Isaiah
A Guide to Acts
A Guide to Romans
A Guide to 1 Corinthians
A Guide to Philippians
Church History
A Guide to Religions

TEF Study Guide 4

A GUIDE TO THE BOOK OF AMOS

with Theme Discussions on
Judgement : Social Justice : Priest and Prophet

BERNARD THOROGOOD

PUBLISHED IN
ASSOCIATION WITH THE
UNITED SOCIETY FOR CHRISTIAN LITERATURE
FOR THE
THEOLOGICAL EDUCATION FUND

LONDON
S·P·C·K
1971

First published in 1971
by the S.P.C.K.
Holy Trinity Church
Marylebone Road, London, NW1 4DU

Made and Printed in Great Britain by
Willmer Brothers Limited, Birkenhead

SBN 281 02592 4

Contents

The photographs in this book are reproduced by courtesy of the U.S.C.L. (on p. 97) and of Camera Press Ltd.

"I will send a fire . . . and it shall devour the strongholds."

The design on the cover is based on part of a stone-carving made during the reign of Tiglath-Pileser III to commemorate the Assyrians' conquest of the hill city Ashteroth-Karnaim, which may be the Karnaim mentioned in Amos 6.13.

Editor's Note: Using this Guide

Before starting to work with this Guide, readers may find it helpful to decide how they intend to use it. Some students may be able to devote less time than others to the study of Amos. Some teachers may consider the social, political, and economic implications of Amos's message, as well as its theological teaching, so important that they prefer to set the book as a text for a course in practical theology or ethics, rather than Old Testament. In either case, they may wish to use the Guide selectively.

The Introduction (pp. 1–8) provides some historical information about Israel at the time of Amos, and about the prophets who preceded him, together with notes about how the Book of Amos came to be written. It includes a *map* of Israel, Judah, and the neighbouring nations (p. 2), and a *time chart* showing comparative dates of kings and prophets in the two Israelite kingdoms (p. 6). Some students will wish to read this Introduction carefully, and carry out the further study suggested, before they begin to study the Bible text itself. Some may wish to read it through quickly and then go straight on to the Book of Amos. Others may wish to *start* by studying the first one or two chapters of Amos with the help of the Guide, and then go back to the Introduction for fuller background information.

The Guide itself is divided into five *Parts*. Each of these covers one or two chapters, and consists of:

—a short Introductory outline, in which the passage is summarized and its relationship to other parts of the Book explained;

—two or more sections, each divided into

(a) *Summary and Background* to the prophet's message and teaching as contained in the passage,

(b) *Detailed Interpretation* of the passage and commentary *Notes* on particular words and phrases requiring explanation, with some discussion of the meaning of Amos's message for today, and

(c) *Study Suggestions.*

Three Theme Discussions have been added, following Parts I, II, and IV. In these, three important subjects of Amos's preaching: judgement, social justice, and religious tradition, are treated more fully, particularly with regard to their practical implications for

Christians at the present time. Some readers may not share the views expressed in these discussions, nor agree with all the interpretations given of the words of Amos. The author has taken pains to mention the major questions relating to Amos or his Book on which biblical scholars differ or are undecided; but it seemed right that these theme studies should reflect a single consistent point of view, not least in order to stimulate thought and provoke discussion. Students whose time is limited, or who are chiefly concerned to understand the words of Amos in the context of Old Testament history and religion, may decide to ignore these discussions and use only the "commentary" sections of the Guide; others may like to use them as "supplementary" reading.

The Study Suggestions appear at the end of each section within the Introduction and Parts, and at the end of each Theme Discussion. They are intended to help readers who are working alone to study more thoroughly and understand the message of Amos more clearly, and to check their own progress. They also provide topics for group research and discussion. They relate to:

1. *Words.* These are to help readers to check and to deepen their understanding of some important words and phrases.
2. *Content.* These questions will help a reader to check his progress and ensure he has fully grasped the ideas and points of teaching studied.
3. *Bible.* These provide an opportunity to compare these ideas and teaching with teaching found in other parts of the Bible.
4. *Application, Opinion, Research.* These suggestions will help readers to think out and discuss the practical application of the truths and teaching in the Book of Amos to everyday life, both as individuals and as members of society.

The best way to use these Study Suggestions is: *first*, read the Bible passage itself; *secondly,* read the appropriate section of the Guide carefully once or twice; and *lastly* do the work suggested, in writing or group discussion, without looking at the Guide again except when there is an instruction to do so.

Please note that all these suggestions are only *suggestions*. Some readers may not want to use them at all. Some teachers may wish to select only those which are relevant to a particular situation, or may prefer to substitute alternative questions of their own.

The Key at the end of the book (p. 111) will enable readers to check their own work on those questions which can be checked in this way. In most cases the Key does not give the answer to a question: it shows where an answer is to be found, either in the Guide or in the Bible.

The Index includes only the more important proper names of people and places, and the main subjects which occur in the Book of Amos or which are discussed in the Guide.

Bible Version. The English translation of the Bible used and quoted in this Guide is the Revised Standard Version of the Bible. The New English Bible is quoted in one or two cases where it helps to show the meaning of a particular passage, and occasional reference is made to the Authorized or King James Version.

Abbreviations. The following abbreviations are used in the Guide:

AV	Authorized Version
B.C.	Before Christ
Chron.	Chronicles
Col.	Colossians
Cor.	Corinthians
Dan.	Daniel
Deut.	Deuteronomy
Eccles.	Ecclesiastes
e.g.	for example
Eph.	Ephesians
Exod.	Exodus
Ezek.	Ezekiel
Gal.	Galatians
Gen.	Genesis
Hag.	Haggai
Heb.	Hebrews
Hos.	Hosea
i.e.	that is
Isa.	Isaiah
Jas.	James
Jer.	Jeremiah
Jon.	Jonah
Josh.	Joshua
Lev.	Leviticus
Mal.	Malachi
Matt.	Matthew
Mic.	Micah
NEB	New English Bible
Neh.	Nehemiah
Num.	Numbers
Obad.	Obadiah
p., pp.	page, pages
Pet.	Peter
Phil.	Philippians
Prov.	Proverbs
Ps. Pss.	Psalm, Psalms
Rev.	Revelation
RSV	Revised Standard Version
Rom.	Romans
Sam.	Samuel
Thess.	Thessalonians
Tim.	Timothy
U.S.A.	United States of America
v., vv.	verse, verses
Zech.	Zechariah
Zeph.	Zephaniah

Bibliography

Readers may find the following books useful for further study of the Book of Amos.

INTRODUCTORY BOOKS:

Amos, T. C. Witney and B. F. Price, Christian Literature Society (Christian Students' Library), Madras

Amos and Micah, J. Marsh, SCM Press, London. A short commentary with excellent theological interpretations.

Hosea to Jonah, J. Myers, SCM Press, London. A full commentary for the non-expert.

The Minor Prophets, H. R. Boer, Daystar, Ibadan. A simplified version of the book by G. L. Robinson, *The Twelve Minor Prophets.*

The Relevance of the Prophets, R. B. Y. Scott, Macmillan, London. For general introduction to prophecy.

MORE ADVANCED BOOKS

Interpreter's Bible, Vol. 6, Abingdon-Cokesbury, New York. Both introduction and commentary on Amos.

Peake's Commentary on the Bible (1962 Edition), Nelson, London. Section on Amos.

The Book of the 12 Prophets, Vol. 1, G. Adam Smith, Hodder and Stoughton, London. A wonderful old commentary which the serious student should buy, beg, or borrow.

The Hebrew Kingdoms, E. W. Heaton, OUP, London.

The Latter Prophets, T. Henshaw, Allen and Unwin, London. Useful introduction.

The Message of the Prophets, G. von Rad, SCM Press, London. Useful background.

INTRODUCTION

"The words of Amos . . . which he saw concerning Israel"

1. THE NATIONS

ISRAEL AND JUDAH

After the death of King Solomon, about the year 930 B.C., the kingdom of Israel was divided into two. The tribes of Judah and Benjamin in the south remained loyal to the new king, Rehoboam, the son of Solomon. The other tribes in the north revolted under the leadership of Jeroboam, a man who had been one of Solomon's lieutenants, and made him their king. From that time the southern kingdom was called Judah, while the northern kingdom kept the name Israel. They were both small kingdoms, rather like some of the African chiefdoms or Indian princedoms in more recent times. Their people were mostly farmers and traders, and they had none of the power of modern "nations".

Israel and Judah were very closely related. The people of both tribes spoke the same language, honoured the same ancestors, and followed many of the same customs. People could travel easily from one kingdom to the other. But there was often trouble and bitterness between them. One reason for this was that they had different forms of worship. For the people of Judah their capital city of Jerusalem was the chief place of worship; the temple there was their "holy place". But for the people of Israel, the altars at Bethel and Gilgal were more important, where idols had been set up by the rebel king Jeroboam. The two nations were also separated by political differences. Israel looked to the north, and tried to find allies among the nations there. Judah looked to the south, and hoped that Egypt would be her friend. (See map p. 2.)

The capital town of Israel was Samaria. During the time of Amos many rich people were living there. Some of these people had probably gained their wealth by leasing or selling their land to working farmers. Others were merchants who bought and sold the produce of the hillside farms. But there were also many people in Samaria who were very poor. Sometimes the harvests failed. Then the farmers got into debt to the traders, and the traders treated them very harshly.

The king of Israel at the time of Amos was Jeroboam II (we read about his reign in 2 Kings 14.23–29). Politically he was a

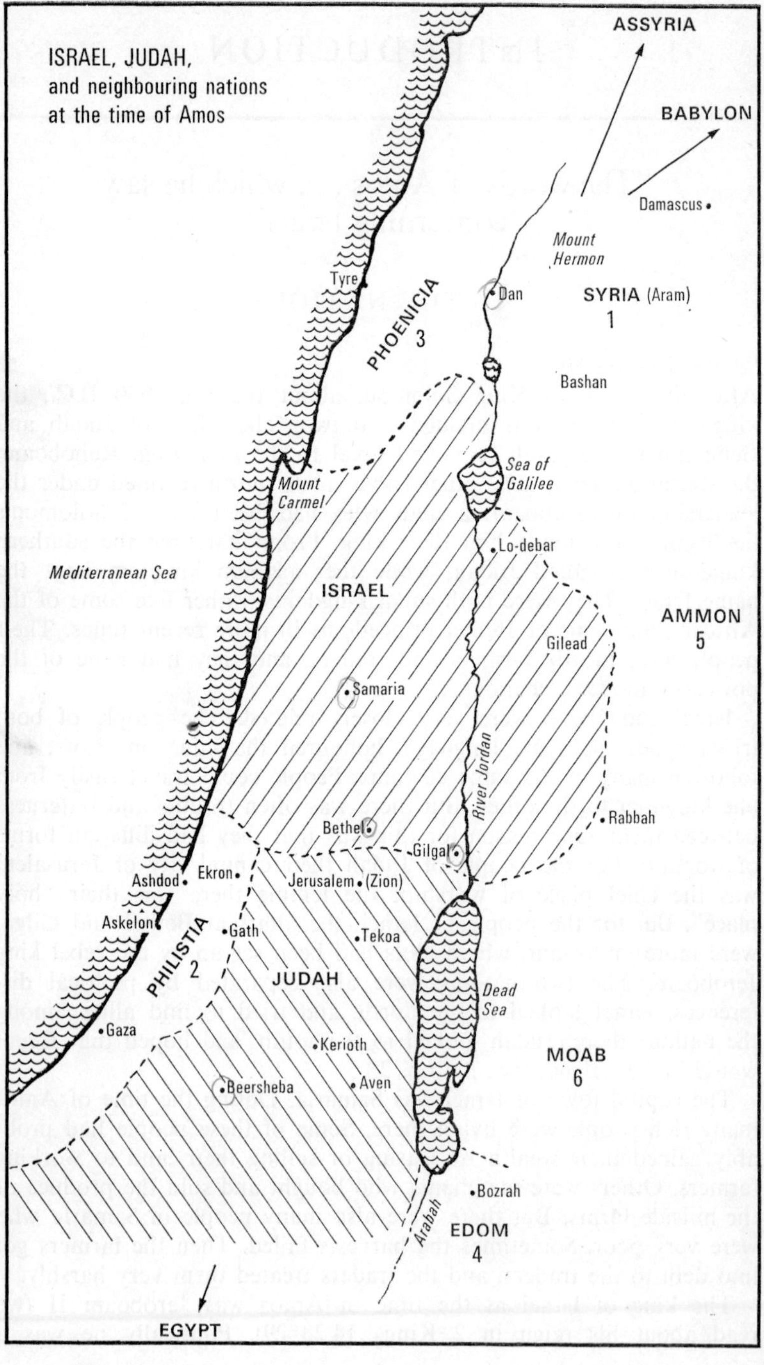
ISRAEL, JUDAH,
and neighbouring nations
at the time of Amos
ASSYRIA
BABYLON
Damascus
Mount Hermon
Tyre
Dan
SYRIA (Aram)
1
PHOENICIA
3
Bashan
Sea of Galilee
Mount Carmel
Lo-debar
Mediterranean Sea
ISRAEL
AMMON
5
Gilead
Samaria
River Jordan
Rabbah
Bethel
Gilgal
Ashdod
Ekron
Jerusalem (Zion)
Askelon
Gath
Tekoa
PHILISTIA
2
JUDAH
Dead Sea
Gaza
Kerioth
MOAB
6
Beersheba
Aven
Bozrah
Arabah
EDOM
4
EGYPT

strong ruler, and during his reign the people felt secure. They could see the boundaries of their nation being extended to the north-east. But they failed to see the great danger which was coming from Assyria, further to the north—a danger which Amos saw very clearly.

ASSYRIA

Some of the nations surrounding Israel and Judah were large, with big armies; some were small and weak. At the time when Amos lived, the kingdom of Assyria was the most aggressive and powerful of these nations. The Assyrians were a fierce and warlike people. They had become powerful in the ninth century B.C., and ruled the whole stretch of land between the Mediterranean coast north of Palestine and the river Tigris at Nineveh. In 841 B.C. the king of Assyria, Shalmaneser III, invaded Syria and compelled Jehu, who was then king of Israel, to pay him large sums of tribute money. It was clear to the people of Israel that they could not fight against Assyria with any hope of success.

But the Assyrians themselves had problems. Their nation covered a wide area which included many different tribes of people. During the period from 800 B.C. to 750 B.C. the tribes in the northern part of this Assyrian empire were restless, and eager to rebel. The Assyrians therefore concentrated their armies in that area, and Israel had a period of safety. But when Tiglath-Pileser III became king of Assyria in about 745 B.C. there was no more rest for Israel. He was a great soldier and conquered many territories. He occupied Damascus in 732 B.C., and this led to the fall of Samaria some years later, in 721 B.C. That was the end of Israel as a separate kingdom. The Assyrians took large numbers of Israelites away from their land, and completely broke up their national life.

OTHER NATIONS AND TRIBES

The map on p. 2 shows the nations bordering Israel. Syria (marked 1 on the map) was perhaps the strongest of these. Its capital city, Damascus, remains today as the capital of the modern nation of Syria. The boundary between Israel and Syria was not clearly fixed, and there were frequent disputes about it. During the time when Jehu was king of Israel (841–814 B.C.), the king of Syria, Hazael, had been able to conquer part of Israel. As a result of this, Jehu's son Jehoahaz (814–798 B.C.) was for much of his reign under the power of the kings of Syria, first Hazael and then his son, Benhadad (see 2 Kings 13.1–9). Assyria then attacked Syria; Israel was able to win back its land (see Amos 1.3–4), and for a time, as we have seen, remained at peace.

Note that Syria (which was also called Aram, the land of the Aramaeans) and Assyria were two separate nations. As we have seen, the Assyrians conquered the Syrian capital city, Damascus, in 732, and for a time the country of Syria became part of the Assyrian empire.

Two other important nations were Philistia (2) and Phoenicia (3). They were both coastal nations, and they had become rich through their trade with other countries around the Mediterranean. Their people worshipped idols.

Edom (4), Ammon (5), and Moab (6) were much poorer nations. They had a few settled towns, but their people were mostly nomads who gained a hard living in very infertile country. They were constantly looking at the rich Jordan valley with envious eyes.

STUDY SUGGESTIONS

WORDS

1. In this Introduction the following words are used:
 (a) nation (b) tribe (c) kingdom (d) empire
 Explain the meaning of each, and illustrate your answer with present-day examples.

CONTENT

2. (a) Why did the kingdom of Israel become divided after the death of Solomon?
 (b) What were the names of:
 (i) the northern kingdom, and (ii) its capital city?
 (iii) the southern kingdom, and (iv) its capital city?
 (c) Name (i) two things which connected the two Israelite kingdoms and (ii) two things which divided them.
3. (a) What was the difference between Syria and Assyria?
 (b) Which king of Assyria conquered Damascus in:
 (i) 841 B.C.? (ii) 732 B.C.?
4. (a) Which of the following were rich nations, and which were poor nations?
 (i) Philistia (ii) Ammon (iii) Moab (iv) Phoenicia (v) Edom
 (b) Why were the rich nations rich?
 (c) Why were the poor nations poor?
5. Of which nation was Damascus the capital?
6. (a) Of which nations were Hazael and Benhadad kings?
 (b) Who was king of Israel at the time when Amos was preaching?

APPLICATION, OPINION, RESEARCH

7. Draw an outline map of Palestine, including the River Jordan, the Dead Sea, and the Sea of Galilee. Mark the positions of

Samaria and Jerusalem. From Samaria draw lines with arrow-heads pointing in the approximate direction of:
(a) Egypt (b)Assyria (c) Moab (d) Syria (e) Philistia (f) Ammon.

8. Imagine that you are king of Israel in the year 750 B.C. What would you decide to do: lead your people into battle against Syria? Persuade neighbouring nations to help you? Or take some other action, and if so, what action? Give reasons for your answer.

2. THE PROPHETS

THE WORK OF A PROPHET

Amos is sometimes called the first of the prophets of Israel. It is true that he was the earliest of a great line of men, the prophets of the Lord who lived in the eighth century B.C. Soon after his time Hosea, Micah, and Isaiah were at work. But Amos was not the first prophet Israel had ever known. There had been great preachers before him. We can trace the history of prophecy in Israel right back to Moses, who was able to speak with authority because he had received from God words of great power. The work of a prophet is never easy. The people of Israel often felt that Moses spoke to them more sternly than they deserved. But Moses was not concerned about his own sternness, nor about the Israelites' feelings. He had experienced the holiness and power of God in his heart, and he felt compelled to speak the words he had received from Him.

Another group of men had begun to prophesy some centuries earlier, in the eleventh century B.C., during the time of Samuel. And for a long period there continued to be groups of religious men or members of particular families in Israel, who were called "sons of the prophets". Not much is known about their activities, but they seem to have joined in excited speaking, singing, and dancing, and they probably studied the Law together.

We learn from the New Testament that the coming of the Holy Spirit gave unusual powers to some of the early Christians, and among these powers was that of "speaking with tongues" (1 Cor. 14.2). The "sons of the prophets" may have felt something of that sort of power. However, when Paul wrote to the Corinthians, he reminded them that love is a greater gift of the Spirit than speaking with tongues. And the excitement experienced by the "sons of the prophets" was certainly less important than the message handed down by the prophets of the Lord. But even though we may not see much value in the work which the "sons of the prophets" did, we can be sure that they had a serious purpose, and that they helped to remind the Israelites of the glory and power of God.

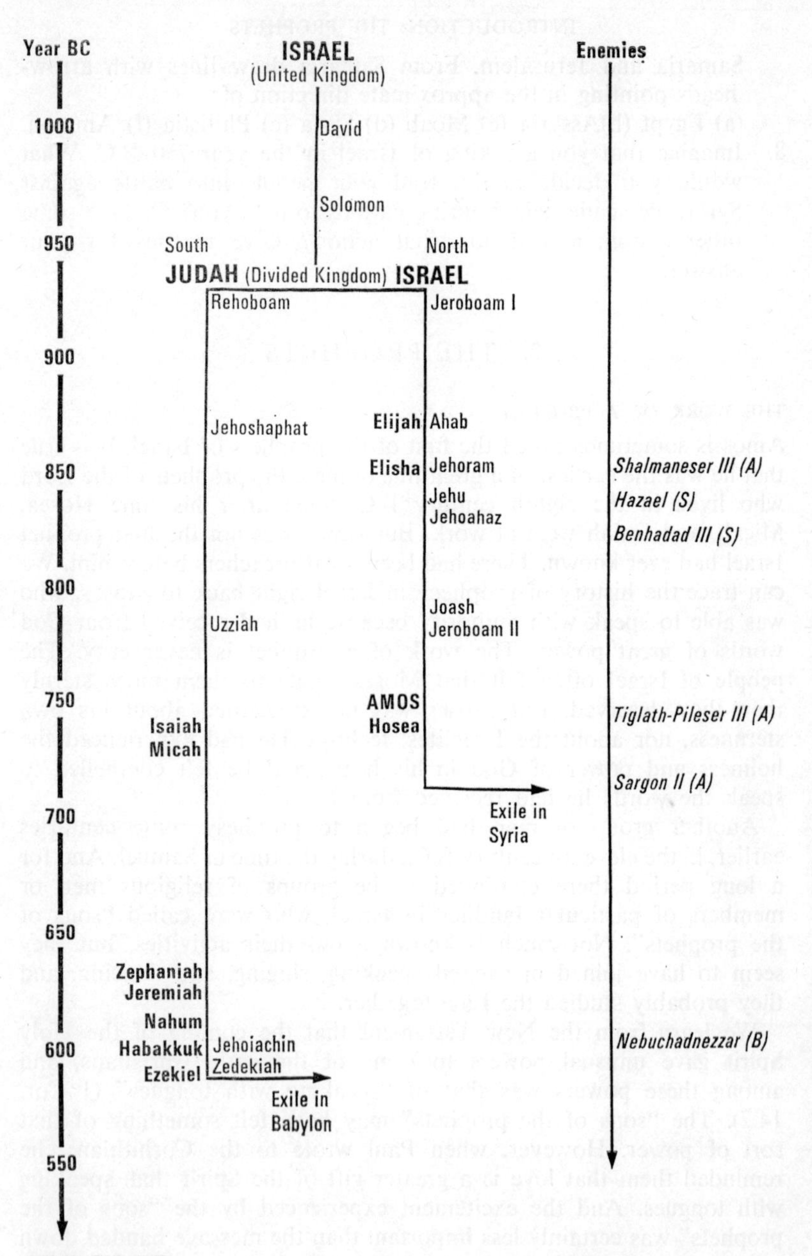

TIME CHART

Showing comparative dates of kings and prophets in the two Israelite kingdoms, and of the kings of enemy countries: Assyria (A), Syria (S), and Babylon (B), whose names are mentioned in the Guide.

Two more important men in the line of prophets were Elijah and Elisha, who lived in the ninth century B.C. They were both deeply concerned that the Israelites should be faithful to God in their life and worship. Sometimes they preached; sometimes they showed their message through their actions. They were courageous men, and were ready to stand alone at a time when the Israelites were being led into the sin of Baal-worship and were taking part in the pagan Canaanites' worship of idols.

Thus Amos had behind him a long history of holy men who had spoken the message they had received from God, and whose words helped to give an answer to the questions "Who is God?", "What is God like?", and "How should people serve Him?" These are questions which people of all nations, and at all times, have asked. The prophets were reminding the Israelites that, for them, the answers were to be found in the Covenant which God had made with Moses. Christians believe that these questions are *fully* answered only in the life, death, and resurrection of Jesus.

THE IMPORTANCE OF AMOS

Although there had been many prophets before him, Amos was the first of the group known as the eighth century prophets. They are especially important because:

(a) their words are preserved for us in much greater detail than the words of earlier preachers (and for this reason they are sometimes called the "writing prophets", though they did not write down their own words themselves);

(b) their words have great power, and are often in the form of memorable poetry;

(c) their words show that they had a deep understanding of the ways of God and His will for men;

(d) their words show also that they had an insight into the hearts and minds of the Israelites at that time.

Another feature of their preaching which we should notice is their ability to look forward into the future. Many people today use the word "prophet" to mean only one thing: a man who can predict or foretell the future, one who "tells fortunes". But prediction was not the chief purpose of any of the eighth century prophets. When they spoke of the future it was in order to show people what the results of their behaviour or belief would be. The prophets saw very clearly that many of the events in people's lives do not happen simply by chance. What we do at any particular time will inevitably affect our situation in the future. The prophets also believed that it is not human beings alone who shape the future. God also is active in the world. So when they preached they could not avoid speaking of the future, because they saw the future results of events just as clearly as they saw the events themselves. The prophets' purpose, however, was not to "tell fortunes". They did not care if their message was unpopular with the people. Their purpose was to change people's hearts and persuade them to change their ways, so that the future might bring a blessing and not a punishment from God.

These prophets of the Lord, then, were holy men who spoke with power. When we say that they were "holy" we mean that they were fully committed to the service of God. They were faithful to God, and called others to be faithful to Him also. They were ready to fight as God's soldiers in the war against all that was evil in the world. They spoke with power because they were sure that God was calling them to speak. They were not offering advice which might or might not be true. They were ready to risk their lives because they believed that God had shown them what they must say to His people.

STUDY SUGGESTIONS

WORDS

1. (a) For each of the words in line (i) below, choose a word from line (ii) which has the same or nearly the same meaning:
   (i) inspire explain proclaim examine foretell instruct
   (ii) expound inspect declare teach empower predict
   (b) Which *three* of the words in line (i) above would you most want to use in order to describe the work of a prophet?
2. Give examples from everyday life to show the difference in meaning between the following words:
   preaching prophecy prediction
3. The words "prophecy" and "prophesy" are used in this section. Write a sentence using both words in such a way as to show the difference between them.

CONTENT

4. Who were the "sons of the prophets"?
5. (a) To what group of prophets did Amos belong?
   (b) Name three other men who prophesied soon after the time of Amos.
   (c) Give three reasons why this group of prophets is especially important.
   (d) For what two reasons did this group of prophets speak of the future?

BIBLE

6. There are many passages in the Bible which tell us some truth about the prophets of Israel, e.g. from Amos 5.8 we learn that

when a prophet received a message from God he felt compelled to deliver it to his people. What general truths about the prophets do the following passages contain?
(a) Num. 24.13 (b) Deut. 34.10–12 (c) 1 Sam. 9.5–17
(d) 2 Kings 17.13, 14 (e) Isa. 3.15 (f) Jer. 1.7–9 (g) Jer. 28.15, 16

OPINION

7. "The prophets ... did not care if their message was unpopular with the people." (p. 8). The English word popular is derived from the Latin *popularis* meaning "of or belonging to the people". Thus to be "unpopular" is to speak or behave differently from the people, i.e. in a way that is not pleasing to them.
   (a) What gave the prophets the "power" to preach an unpopular message?
   (b) In your experience, do Christian preachers today often preach a message which is unpopular?
   (c) Did Jesus often preach an unpopular message?
   Give examples to support your answers to (b) and (c).
8. Many people today use the word "prophet" to mean only "a person who can foretell the future".
   (a) Do people in your country use the word "prophet" in this way? If not, for what sort of person do they use it?
   (b) Do you think that God intends us to know the future? Give reasons for your answer.

3. THE WORDS OF AMOS

THE MAN

Not very much is known about the life of Amos. All that we do know is found in the book itself. Amos had lived at Tekoa, a small town in Judah near Bethlehem (Amos 1.1 and 7.12). It is clear that he had worked as a shepherd (1.1) or a herdsman (7.14). He may also have been an expert fruit-grower, since he spoke of himself as a "dresser" of sycamore trees, which gave an edible fruit rather like a fig. He had lived and worked in the country, not in a city. He came from his farming work to be a prophet to the people of Israel. Because he came from the countryside, where everyone had to work hard for a living, he was disgusted to see the wealth, the laziness, and the unjust behaviour of some of the town dwellers in the northern kingdom. Amos did not belong to a priestly or prophetic family (7.14 and see p. 84); he became a prophet because he experienced the calling of God.

The Book of Amos shows that he was a powerful preacher. His language was vivid, full of epigrams and brief word-pictures. Amos was not shy about using strong words when he felt that they were needed. He called the rich women of Samaria "You cows of Bashan" (4.1). He did not apologize for his message, or try to make his words pleasing to his hearers. He was forthright and made his message very clear. He used his own experience in the rough countryside to illustrate his teaching (3.4–5), but he was not an ignorant peasant. He probably travelled to the market towns to sell his wool and fruit, and it is likely that he met travellers from other countries. He certainly knew something of the history of the Philistines and the Syrians (see 9.7), and had heard about the annual flooding of the River Nile (see 8.8 and 9.5).

THE BOOK

The Book of Amos is a collection of the prophet's words. We cannot be certain who actually wrote it, or when it was written. Most scholars think it is unlikely that Amos wrote down anything himself or dictated his message to a secretary as the prophet Jeremiah did (Jer. 36.4). During the lifetime of Amos people probably remembered his words because they were so clear and strong. Then, when he had finished speaking, or when he died, those who admired his words would want to keep them from being forgotten. A number of people each wrote down what he remembered. Probably these small pieces of writing were circulated among the friends and followers of Amos, and later they were collected together.

Scholars today study carefully the form and language of the different parts of the Book of Amos, and can suggest how the various sayings of the prophet were brought together, so as to make one "book". Although these are only suggestions, they do help us to understand the plan of the book as a whole. Here are some of them:

(a) The section from Amos 7.1 to 8.3 is very personal. It is a record of words which the prophet spoke about himself. The "visions" described in this section were not public; they were a personal experience, in which Amos understood God's word to him. In the book, the visions are placed before and after the section 7.10–14, which records an event in Amos's ministry and contains the prophet's own descriptions of his call by God. For this reason, most scholars think that the visions were a part of that call. They think that this was the experience in which God was saying to Amos "Go, prophesy". If this suggestion is correct, then the visions occurred before Amos preached the stern message contained in chapters 1 to 6.

(b) Chapters 1 and 2 form the longest connected passage in the book. It seems likely that this was a single discourse or "sermon" which Amos preached at the start of his ministry. Perhaps he preached it more than once, so that the words remained in the memory of his hearers.

(c) The verses 3.1, 4.1, and 5.1 each begin with the phrase "Hear this word" as an introduction to the sayings which follow. This may be the way in which Amos usually began his preaching. But in each of these chapters the sayings are short ones, not continuous passages. It therefore seems likely that the later "editors" of the book used the introductory verses as a way of making clear to readers that these sayings were spoken in public by the prophet.

(d) 8.4–14 contains much the same kind of message as chapters 2 and 3. Some scholars have suggested that in its earliest form the Book of Amos contained only the two parts which appear as 7.1—8.3, and 8.4–14 in the present book; that is, the personal material, and then a summary of the prophet's message. This small collection may have been written down shortly after the actual ministry of Amos, even before the fall of Samaria.

(e) A larger book may have been put together after Israel and many of the other nations had been defeated by the Assyrians. It may have been the work of men in the remaining kingdom of Judah, who saw that many of the disasters which Amos foretold had actually occurred. So they wrote down the warnings he had given, and placed these at the start of the book as chapters 1 to 6, adding 1.1, which gives the date according to the kings of Judah, and 2.4–5, which brings Judah into the list of nations condemned.

(f) During the Exile of Judah in Babylon the book was probably revised again, and further additions made to it. There are reasons for believing that 4.13; 5.8, 9; 9.5, 6; and 9.11–15 were added at this later period, since the language and style of these verses are similar to those of the prophets who were preaching at that time.

Students who are interested in the historical development of the Book of Amos can follow up these brief notes in any of the more advanced Introductions to the Prophetic works. Although the suggestions of the scholars cannot be proved, yet they are very helpful in understanding the collection of sayings that makes up a single book of the Bible. It becomes clear to us that, although it is probable that not every word of the book is exactly as spoken by Amos, yet the book as a whole preserves the basic message of the prophet for us. Those who made the book were men who were influenced by the preaching of Amos and who honoured his message.

THE MESSAGE

The message which Amos preached was an unpopular one. The Israelites were accustomed to thinking that they were the chosen people of God, and Amos, too, acccepted this. He believed that God and Israel were bound together by the Covenant which God had made with Moses at Sinai (Amos 3.1–2). God had promised to care for the Israelites and save them from their enemies if they would follow the way of life which He laid down for them. The Israelites for their part had promised: "All the words which the Lord has spoken we will do" (Exod. 24.5).

This special relationship with God had given the people of Israel special opportunities for understanding what God is like and how people ought to serve Him. But when Amos looked at his fellow Israelites he saw that these special opportunities had not led to special righteousness. Instead, he saw the Israelites breaking their promise to God, and behaving as though the law which He had laid down for them did not exist. ("They have rejected the law of the Lord, and have not kept his statutes" Amos 2.4.)

Amos accused the Israelites of two sorts of "transgression": (1) injustice to one another, and (2) worship of idols. He preached the stern message that if the Israelites continued to behave in this way, then they could not expect to receive the great blessings which God had promised in His Covenant with them (Exod. 34). Amos saw that the little kingdom of Israel was in no condition to resist attack by Assyria, and would be destroyed; yet he pleaded for a change of heart. Even when he was speaking sternly, he continued to hope that a few people would be saved out of the disasters which were to come. We find an expression of this hope in 5.15. "It may be that the Lord, the God of hosts, will be gracious to the remnant of Joseph." And those scholars who think that 9.11–15 is a record of Amos's own words, and not the work of a later editor, believe that this passage also shows that the message of Amos was one of encouragement as well as warning.

Amos foresaw disaster for some of the surrounding nations, but he was speaking chiefly to his own people, the Israelites. Yet his message has meaning for us also. It is an important message for us today for several reasons:

(a) the God whom Amos proclaimed is the same God whom we worship today through Jesus Christ;

(b) Christian people are bound to God in the New Covenant made by Jesus, and therefore have special responsibilities, just as the Israelites had special responsibilities under the Old Covenant;

(c) we too need to examine ourselves, and our Churches and societies and nations, and to guard against social injustice and idolatrous worship;

(d) even more than in Amos's time, there is a danger that great nations will destroy their smaller neighbours.

Amos preached with passion in his heart, and we should not treat the Book of Amos as though it were a classroom lecture. Amos was calling upon his hearers to respond, and challenging them either to accept or to reject the word of God. He offers the same challenge to all who read the book today.

STUDY SUGGESTIONS

WORDS

1. Amos accused Israel and the other nations of "transgressions". Which *four* of the following words have the same or almost the same meaning as transgression?
   iniquity defence sin omission offencc trcspass rcprcssion

CONTENT

2. Read Amos 1.1 and 7.14, 15
   (a) What part of Palestine did Amos come from?
   (b) What was his trade before he became a prophet?
3. What do we learn about Amos from the following passages?
   (a) Amos 3.4–5; (b) 4.1; (c) 7.14; (d) 9.5 and 7.
4. Who wrote the Book of Amos?
5. Read the following passages: Amos 4.13; 5.8, 9; 9.5, 6 and 11–15. For what reasons do scholars think that these passages may have been added to the book by a later editor?
6. For what two sorts of "transgression" did Amos chiefly accuse the Israelites?
7. Give chapter and verse references for two passages in the Book of Amos which can be taken to show that the prophet's message was one of encouragement as well as warning.

BIBLE

8. Read the following passages, and say in each case what answer the prophet was giving to the question, "Who is God and what is He like?"
   (a) Exod. 34.47 (b) Isa. 6.1–4 (c) Isa. 40.31 (d) Isa. 45.5, 6 (e) Jer. 27.4–5 (f) Amos 7.2, 3 (g) Mal. 2.4–5

APPLICATION, OPINION, RESEARCH

9. "The message of Amos is an important message for us today." (p. 12). Give three reasons why it is important for us, with examples from everyday life to support your answer.
10. If Amos were preaching in your country now, of what sorts of "transgression", if any, do you think he would accuse:
    (a) the political leaders of the nation?
    (b) the leaders of the Church?
    (c) the ordinary people of the country?

STUDY GUIDE AND COMMENTARY

Prologue: Amos and his Message 1.1, 2

SUMMARY AND BACKGROUND

The first two verses of chapter 1 are a sort of introduction to the book. It seems quite certain that the words of verse 1 are not the words of Amos. They were put in by the editors of the book to tell readers who Amos was and when he lived. The names of the kings who are mentioned help us to discover when Amos lived (see the time chart on p. 6). The words "two years before the earthquake" do not help us today, because it is no longer known when this earthquake happened. But for the people who lived closer to the lifetime of Amos, the earthquake was clearly something which they remembered or had heard their parents speak of, so it would help them to fix the date. In the South Pacific islands, people often fix dates by mentioning a hurricane—"That good crop of oranges was two years after the big hurricane"; but that is no help to outsiders who do not know when the hurricane occurred.

NOTES

1.1. The words of Amos ... which he saw: This verse does not explain exactly how Amos received the message from God. But it does make plain that the message was *received,* and not invented by Amos himself. The use of the phrase "he saw" suggests that Amos had a series of visions, which he then described and interpreted for his hearers.

Verse 2 also may have been added by the editors, or it may be an introductory statement used by Amos himself.

1.2. The Lord roars from Zion: This phrase describes in picture-language the message of Amos which follows. The Lord did not speak through Amos in a "still small voice". He spoke with great power, and the message was a message of warning like the crashing of thunder or the roaring of a lion. The name "Zion" is used to emphasize that the message came from the holy place of the Lord, and was to affect the land as far north as Mount Carmel. It was a message for all God's people, for the Israelites of the northern kingdom as well as those in Amos's own country of Judah.

PART I 1.3—2.16
DECLARATION OF GOD'S JUDGEMENT

INTRODUCTION

The first section of the Book of Amos, from 1.3 to 2.16, contains what seems to be the record of a spoken message to the various nations which were threatened by invasion from Assyria or Egypt. Amos was accusing them of failing to keep the laws which God had established for all people. We do not know whether the whole of this message was preached at one time. Some scholars think that the short passages about each nation were spoken at different times, and then collected together later.

There is also some uncertainty about 2.4–5. These verses are spoken to Judah, and Amos did not usually distinguish between Israel and Judah. He regarded them as one family (3.1). For this reason, and also because the language of verse 4 is like the language of much later writings, some scholars think that 2.4–5 are not the words of Amos, but were spoken by some other prophet, or perhaps were added to the book later. Amos was not the only prophet who foresaw that the disobedience of the Israelites and of the other nations would lead to disaster.

1. Judgement against the Nations 1.3—2.3

SUMMARY AND BACKGROUND

Amos began by addressing the nations which surrounded Israel. He said that all these peoples stood in the presence of God; their conduct was not hidden from Him. Amos spoke to each nation in turn, and described their wrongdoings. In each case the national conduct fell short of the standard which God had set for them. In each case, therefore, Amos preached of the judgement and doom that was to come (see Theme Discussion on Judgement, p. 28).

INTERPRETATION AND NOTES

1.3 etc. For three transgressions ... and for four, I will not revoke the punishment: This phrase is repeated for each of the nations.

"For three and for four" does not mean that each nation did wrong exactly three times or four times. It means "a great many", as we might say "dozens" of times. It shows that the nations were not being condemned for a single fault, but for "crime after crime" (NEB), i.e. continuous and repeated sins. The basic meaning of the word "transgression" is "going against". Amos used it here to mean revolt or rebellion against the authority of God. Each nation had broken God's law not once but many times, and Amos believed that the time had come when God would no longer save them from the consequences of their disobedience. (See Theme Discussion on Judgement, p. 29.)

1.3–5. DAMASCUS (SYRIA)

1.3. Threshed Gilead: The repeated sin of Syria was that its army had behaved with great cruelty towards the people of Gilead, in the east of Israel. In those days the Israelites threshed their grain by dragging heavy sledges over piles of corn, so that the stalks were broken up. Verse 3 may be a word-picture of cruel treatment which crushed the Israelites as the threshing sledges crushed the corn. Or it may be that in the fighting the Syrians actually pulled heavy sledges over the bodies of their Israelite captives, and so killed them.

1.4. Hazael and **Benhadad** were kings of Syria, and **Damascus** was its capital city (see Introduction, p. 3). Amos often used the name of a capital city when he really meant the whole country. We have the same custom today, and use phrases like, "Washington claims" or "Moscow denies" in news reports about events in the USA or the Soviet Union.

The "bar" of the city means the gate in the walls. A great bar of wood or iron was used to close the gates. If this bar was broken an enemy could easily enter, so the word was often used to mean the strength or stability of a city.

Amos meant that Syria's "punishment" would be complete defeat in war. The Assyrians would conquer, and take the Syrian people away as captives to Kir, far to the east. This did in fact happen when Tiglath-Pileser conquered Damascus in 732 B.C. (See p. 29, for a note about punishment.)

1.6–10. GAZA . . . TYRE (PHILISTIA AND PHOENICIA)

Philistia (whose capital city was Gaza) had been the enemy of Israel for generations. Phoenicia (whose capital city was Tyre) had been friendly with Israel in the days of Solomon, but by the time Amos was preaching, the friendship had come to an end.

1.6 and 9. A whole people: Amos accused both these nations of the same kind of sin—of carrying off their defeated enemies and selling them as slaves. It was common practice in ancient times for a victorious army to carry away its prisoners of war and sell them as

"Thus says the Lord '. . . I will not revoke the punishment; because they carried into exile a whole people . . . and cast off all pity' " (Amos 1.6, 11).

Women and children are taken away as prisoners, and others are killed, in the war in Vietnam, while the men are in hiding or fighting the enemy.

What sort of "punishment", if any, are modern nations likely to suffer because their armies behave cruelly in war?

slaves. This was one of the dreadful results of war. The same kind of thing still happens today. Those considered to be "enemies of the state" are sentenced to forced labour, and the refugee camps show how a defeated people may lose their land and their homes.

Amos seems to suggest that the Philistines and Phoenicians were specially cruel in the way they carried off not only the defeated soldiers but women and children too. The punishment which Amos foretold was that both these nations would be destroyed in battle. They would receive the same sort of treatment which they had given to others. Amos used the phrase "I will send a fire", for this punishment, and for the punishment of the other nations, because he thought of the attackers setting fire to the cities.

1.11, 12. EDOM

1.11. His brother: There was a tradition among the Israelites that the people of Edom were descended from Esau, the brother of Jacob from whom the Israelites were descended. "There are the descendants of Esau, that is Edom" (Gen. 36.1). For this reason, the Edomites were regarded as being distant cousins of the Israelites. So there ought to have been a brotherly feeling between Edom and Israel, and the phrase "his brother" means Israel. But in fact the feeling between the two nations had always been bad, and the Israelites were sometimes to blame for this. Amos declared that it was wrong to keep up this feud from one generation to another, "for ever". Amos foresaw that Edom also would be punished by being destroyed in war.

1.12. Bozrah was a town in Edom. The site of **Teman** is unknown.

1.13–15. AMMON

The Ammonites were always looking for better land to feed their flocks. So they raided the territory of Gilead, a part of Israel which lay between Ammon and the Jordan valley. Amos declared that the Ammonites carried out these raids with great cruelty, and even killed pregnant women. Once again he foresaw that the punishment would be overwhelming defeat in war.

1.14. Tempest ... whirlwind: Amos may have been remembering the sudden gales which blew out of the southern desert of Judah, and brought dust storms over the land. The Assyrians did come later to attack Ammon with a military assault which was as sudden and overwhelming as a whirlwind.

2.1–3. MOAB

2.1. Burned to lime: When Amos accused Moab he remembered a particular incident which shocked him and his fellow Israelites. The Moabite soldiers had been fighting against Edom, and had dug up the bones of the dead king of Edom and burned them. They must have done this as a sign that the royal family was being completely destroyed. It is interesting to note that in 1917, the communist revolutionaries in Russia not only shot the emperor, Nicholas II, and his family, but also, so far as is known, burned their bodies. On that occasion, also, the purpose must have been to show that the royal family was completely finished for ever.

For many ancient peoples it was a very important custom that the bodies of the dead should not be disturbed in any way, because they believed that the spirit lived on in the corpse. They believed that if the bones were burned, then the spirit of the dead man also would be destroyed. Some peoples still have this custom today. But the fear of burning a dead body is no longer so widespread. It is more widely believed that the spirit is in no way attached to the corpse. But even though this is what Christians believe, most Christians feel it right that a body should be allowed to rest in peace.

Notice that this crime of Moab was not a crime against Israel. It was against Edom. But Amos saw that this was just as bad. God had a special relationship with Israel, but His laws are for *all* people. Again the punishment which Amos foresaw was violent warfare, during which the royal family of Moab would be destroyed. It is not known whether or not this prophecy was fulfilled during the Assyrian attack.

STUDY SUGGESTIONS

WORDS

1. What did Amos mean by the word "transgression" or "crime" (NEB), when he used it to accuse the nations?
2. (a) Which *five* of the following words do *not* have the same meaning as "punishment":
   consequences penalty reckoning chastisement recompense chastity judgement
   (b) What *are* the meanings of each of these five words?

CONTENT

3. What did the editors of the Book of Amos do in order to tell their readers when Amos lived?
4. (a) Of what particular sins did Amos accuse each of the following nations?
   (i) Syria (ii) Edom (iii) Ammon (iv) Moab
   (b) What actions of the Philistines and Phoenicians did Amos consider especially cruel?

5. "The crime of Moab was not a crime against Israel." (p. 19). What do we learn from the fact that, even so, Amos accused Moab in the same way as the other nations?
6. Amos used several different phrases to describe the "punishment" which was to come to the different nations, but there is one phrase which he used for what was to happen to all nations.
   (a) Which is that phrase?
   (b) What did Amos mean by it?

BIBLE

7. "Amos was not the only prophet who saw that the disobedience of the nations would lead to disaster." (p. 15). Read the following passages and say in each case:
   (i) What nation or nations were being accused?
   (ii) In what ways was the disaster or the punishment which the prophet foresaw like or unlike the punishment which Amos foresaw for that nation?
   (a) Isa. 17.1–3 (b) Jer. 48.16–17 (c) Joel 3.4–8 (d) Obad. 1.2, 8–10

APPLICATION, OPINION, RESEARCH

8. "The Edomites were regarded as distant cousins of the Israelites. So there should have been brotherly feelings between Edom and Israel." (p. 18)
   (a) Name any nations or tribes which you know of today, which are descended, like Israel and Edom, from the same ancestors.
   (b) Do they act in a brotherly way towards each other? If not, why is there enmity between them?
9. "For many ancient peoples it was the custom that bodies of the dead should not be disturbed." (p. 19)
   (a) What was the reason for this custom?
   (b) Is the custom still observed today in your country, or in any country which you know, and if so, for what reasons?
   (c) What is your own opinion in the matter?
10. Read the headlines in any recent copy of a newspaper.
   (a) See how many of them refer to conduct by present-day nations which is like the behaviour for which Amos condemned the nations of his time.
   (b) Say in each case what "punishment", if any, seems likely to be the result of such behaviour.

2. Judgement against the Israelites 2.4–16

SUMMARY AND BACKGROUND

The words of Amos recorded in 1.1 – 2.3 must have been quite acceptable to his hearers. No doubt they enjoyed hearing stern accusations against their unfriendly neighbours. This kind of speech is always popular, as many modern politicians know quite well. But when Amos spoke the words recorded in 2.4–16, he was not popular with his hearers at all. This time he directed his accusation against his own people, and spoke with equal sternness. A politician, who needs to be popular with his own people, would never dare to speak as Amos did. A prophet dared to accuse his own people only because he tried to obey God.

As we noted on p. 15, 2.4 and 5 may well be a later addition to the book.

INTERPRETATION AND NOTES

2.4–5. JUDAH

2.4. They have rejected the law of the Lord, and have not kept his statutes: God had given His law to Judah and Israel together, as one people, and "with one voice" they had promised to obey. In the years which had passed since Moses received this law at Sinai, it had been interpreted and developed in the teaching of the priests and the elders. For this reason the people of Judah and Israel ought to have known, better than anyone else, the standard of life and worship which God desires. But most of them had not even tried to reach that standard, and so they could not escape the results of their failure.

Their lies: The last part of verse 4 is not very clear. One possible meaning might be, "The idols which they worship, and which their forefathers copied from the Canaanites, have led them astray."

In verse 5 the punishment of Judah is foreseen. But it was not the Assyrians who were to destroy Jerusalem; the "fire" did not come until Nebuchadnezzar, ruler of Babylon, attacked the city more than a hundred years later.

2.6–16. ISRAEL

These verses show that Amos spoke to his own people in very strong language. He described their repeated sins and denounced them fearlessly for three kinds of disobedience.

1. **2.7. They ... trample the head of the poor:** Amos began by accusing the Israelites of *injustice and cruelty*. In Old Testament

"They have rejected the law of the Lord . . . they . . . trample the head of the poor into the dust of the earth, and turn aside the way of the afflicted" (Amos 2.4, 7).

Wealthy people in Bombay pay high prices for seats at a brightly-lit cinema, while a poor mother in the same part of the city has no other bed for her babies than the pavement.

What sort of "punishment", if any, are rich people today likely to suffer when they refuse to help their poorer neighbours?

times the existence of slavery itself was not condemned as being against God's will. The Israelites had special laws about the way in which slaves should be treated, but slavery was regarded as a very low and degraded state for men to live in. Normally only enemy prisoners captured in battle were used as slaves. No Israelite would ever have used a fellow Israelite as a slave. But Amos pointed out that what was actually happening in Israel was just as bad.

2.6, 7. The righteous and **the needy, the poor** and **the afflicted** were as completely under the power of the rich as if they had in fact been slaves. This was chiefly because the poor people got into debt which they could not repay. Then the merchants and landowners made them work like slaves and treated them very harshly. We should note that this is always a danger in any country where the methods of justice are weak, or where officials can be bribed.

2. **2.7, 8. The same maiden ... beside every altar:** the second part of v. 7 and v. 8 are not entirely clear in Hebrew, and scholars have suggested several different interpretations. It seems most probable that Amos was referring to the custom of "temple prostitution", which was widely practised in Old Testament times. He was accusing the Israelites of *taking part in pagan worship.* Many of the pagan peoples believed that the gods or spirits which they worshipped could control the fertility of the earth, and of human beings and animals. They regarded the sexual act as a sign of fertility, and it was their custom to perform such acts as part of their worship at a shrine or temple. They believed that this would please the gods, and thus ensure good harvests and large families.

This practice was forbidden to the Israelites ("There shall be no cult prostitute among the daughters of Israel, neither ... of the sons of Israel," Deut. 23.17). And it had become debased among the Canaanites and Phoenicians. This was one of the reasons why Amos was warning the Israelites against joining in pagan worship. He probably regarded the "temple prostitution" of his time as a much more serious sin than the ordinary "trade" of prostitution which has continued throughout history.

The people of some religions do not think it very wrong to have sexual intercourse for money. But the Church has always taught that it is wrong for Christians. Jesus taught that all human beings, men and women alike, are equally loved by God and equally precious to Him. He treated slaves and prostitutes as if they were His brothers and sisters, and showed that it is wrong to treat any human being as a thing to be bought and sold for cash.

However, Amos was not thinking about ordinary prostitution or how women should be treated. He was simply accusing the Israelites of imitating the pagan practice of prostitution within the holy places. He saw this as a proof that they were being unfaithful to the

Covenant. God had shown what sort of worship was pleasing to Him, but the Israelites were following pagan ways instead.

2.8. Garments ... wine: Amos may possibly have meant certain kinds of offering which the poorer people made to the priests in the holy places. But it seems more likely that he was referring to the wrongful use of goods which had been taken from the poor instead of payment, or as "pledges" that they would pay off their debts in the future (see Exod. 22.26, 27).

In either case, the picture which Amos showed was clear. The men who were responsible for justice in Israel were taking bribes. The richer people were oppressing and cheating the poor. And it had become customary among the Israelites to visit the holy places, not in order to worship God, but to indulge in noisy and riotous behaviour which was an insult to Him. This is what is meant by the phrase "my holy name is profaned".

3. **2.10. I brought you up:** After accusing the Israelites of (1) oppressing the poor and (2) taking part in pagan worship, Amos went on to condemn them for (3) *ingratitude to God,* and called on them to remember God's goodness towards them (vv. 9–12). He could not look at the sins of the Israelites in his own day without thinking of all that the Lord had done in the past to save this people from their enemies. In these words he reminded them of the greatest sign of God's care for them, the events of the Exodus.

The land of the Amorite: Another name for the land of Canaan. The Amorites had been living in part of Canaan when the Israelites first approached it from the desert: "The Amorites dwell in the hill country" (Num. 13.29). They seem to have been big and powerful men: "All the people that we saw in it are men of great stature" (Num. 13.32).

2.11. Nazirites: Amos then spoke of a further sign of the blessings of God. God had showed His care for the Israelites not only through the Exodus, when they escaped from captivity in Egypt, but also by calling men to a holy life. Amos mentioned two special groups: "prophets" and "Nazirites". He may have been using the word "prophet" to mean the groups of "sons of the prophets" (see p. 5), who may be compared to the "revivalist" preachers of today. The Nazirites belonged to a group which had been established for many years. Their rules for living are given in Numbers 6. (Note that the Nazirites should not be confused with the Nazarenes, the people of Nazareth.)

The Nazirites and similar Jewish religious groups such as the Rechabites (Jer. 35.6) were rather like the religious orders of monks and nuns in the Christian Church who live according to strict rules of conduct. The great value of religious communities is that they help men and women to dedicate themselves to the service of God. The particular rules which they follow are chiefly ways to learn obedience. Some of these rules have only a temporary and local value; for example, the Rechabites were supposed to live in tents instead of houses, in order to remind them of the Exodus, although stone houses or brick ones were much more suitable for town life.

God calls most people to obey Him without belonging to a religious order. But the offering of life to God is always a sign of the Holy Spirit at work, and Amos rightly saw that such groups of dedicated men were a true gift of God to the people.

The Israelites, however, had rejected these gifts (v. 11). They had made the Nazirites break their vows, and had told the prophets to keep silent. Amos was calling the people to consider what sort of response they were making to the gracious gifts of God.

2.12. I will press you down: Then Amos warned the Israelites of the results of their opposition to God (vv. 13–16). These verses are written in poetical form, as a series of word-pictures showing how the strength of Israel's armies would be turned into weakness. Amos was preaching to a people who thought that they were strong and safe. So he declared that the strength and safety of a people which fights against God are very temporary things.

Other prophets have pointed to the other side of this truth: "He gives power to the faint, and to him who has no might he increases strength" (Isa. 40.29). Those who trust and obey God find that their weakness becomes a lasting strength. We can understand this more clearly if we think of the tiny minorities of Christians in some of the communist countries today, or of the early Church in the Roman Empire. Which had the real and lasting strength, the great pagan nation or the small group of people trying to remain faithful to God? Or to take this even further, think of Caiaphas and Christ: which one of those two was the stronger?

Having studied the first two chapters of Amos we can see that two very important truths are taught here:

1. Amos spoke the word of the Lord, the one Lord God, to *all* the nations. He did not see Israel as under God's hand, while the other peoples were under the idols. God's word applied to them all equally. The fact that the pagan nations did not accept the authority of God did not remove them from that authority. Jesus was teaching this same truth when He said, "the Gospel must be preached to all nations" (Mark 13.10). God, the creator and Lord of all, extends His authority and His love to all peoples of every nation, whatever their race and whatever their religion.

2. We have already noticed the sort of sin for which the various nations were condemned. They can be described as sins against humanity: cruelty, hatred, complete lack of respect for other people.

The pagans were guilty of these sins, just as the Israelites were guilty of injustice to the poor. Amos thus believed that *all* men are responsible to God for their behaviour to one another. As Paul said, "You have no excuse, O man, whoever you are" (Rom. 2.1). God has created us human beings, and in Jésus He has shown us how human beings should behave—not as wild beasts tearing each other to pieces.

STUDY SUGGESTIONS

WORDS

1. In Amos 2.4 the word "statute" is used to mean the law which God had given to his people in the Covenant. Read Psalm 119. 1–8, and list *five* other words which are used there to mean the law of God.
2. The word-picture which Amos used to describe how God destroyed the Amorites was also used by Hosea to describe the disaster which he foresaw for the tribe of Ephraim (Hos. 9.16), and by Bildad to describe the sufferings of the wicked (Job 18.16–19).
   (a) What is that word-picture and what is its meaning?
   (b) Give examples of any other commonly used word-pictures which have the same meaning, in English or in another language.
3. Explain the difference in meaning between "Nazirite" and "Nazarene".

CONTENT

4. "When Amos spoke the words recorded in 2.4–16 he was not popular with his hearers" (p. 21 and see question 7 on p. 9).
   (a) For what reason was he not popular?
   (b) What gave Amos the courage to speak in a way in which no modern politician would dare to speak?
5. "The people of Judah and Israel should have known, better than anyone else, the standard of life and worship which God desires." (p 21) For what reason should they have known better than other nations what God desires?
6. (a) Of what sin did Amos accuse Judah?
   (b) What punishment did he foresee for Judah?
   (c) What did in fact happen to Judah more than a hundred years later?
7. (a) What was the custom referred to in the second part of 2. 7?
   (b) On what pagan belief was this custom based?
   (c) What was the law of Israel in regard to this custom?
8. "Amos was calling on the Israelites to remember God's goodness towards them" and "to consider what sort of response they were making to God's gracious gifts". (pp. 24, 25)

(a) Of which two great examples of God's goodness towards them did Amos remind the Israelites?

(b) In what ways had the Israelites shown that they rejected God's gifts?

9. "In the first two chapters of the Book of Amos two very important truths are taught." (p. 25). What are these two truths?

BIBLE

10. Read:
    (a) Exod. 23.6–8; Isa. 1.23; Amos 2.6
    (b) Exod. 22.21–25; Amos 2.7; Mic. 2.1, 2
    (c) Exod. 22.26, 27; Amos 2.8; Mic. 2.8

    For each of these groups of verses say: (i) What was the law which God had given to His people in the Covenant? (ii) For what sort of behaviour were the prophets denouncing the Israelites?

11. Read the following passages and say:
    (i) Which of them contain the important truth taught by Amos and also by Jesus according to Mark 13.10?
    (ii) Which of them contain the important truth taught by Amos and also by St Paul in Romans 2.1, 2?
    (a) Ps. 15 (b) Isa. 13.11 (c) Isa. 55.5 (d) Dan. 7.13, 14 (e) Mark 4.23–25 (f) Acts 13.47

12. "The Church has always taught that prostitution, i.e. to have sexual intercourse for money, is wrong for Christians." (p. 23). What reasons for this teaching do we find in each of the following passages? (a) Matt. 19.3, 5; (b) Rom. 6.12–14; (c) 1 Cor. 6.15, 16; (d) 1 Cor. 6.19, 20.

APPLICATION, OPINION, RESEARCH

13. Read again Amos 2.13–16
    (a) What sorts of people was Amos describing in vv. 14–16 and what had they in common (besides the disasters which Amos foresaw for them)?
    (b) Rewrite vv. 13–16 in your own words, using modern word-pictures for strength and weakness (e.g. instead of a "cartful of sheaves" you might refer to a bulldozer).

14. "No Israelite would ever have used a fellow-Israelite as a slave." (And no "civilized" people today would ever use their fellow-countrymen as slaves.) "But Amos pointed out that what was actually happening in Israel was just as bad." (p. 23).

    Do you think that anything which is "actually happening" in your own country or other countries today is "just as bad" as slavery? If so, give examples.

15. Read Num. 6 and Jer. 35.6–7 and list the rules for (a) Nazarites, and (b) Rechabites.
    Do you think that Church members should have to obey rules of this sort? Or only small groups of people within the Church? Or do you think that all Christians should be free from such laws about conduct? Give reasons for your answer.
16. (a) What would you reply to someone who said he could not believe that it is possible for God to turn weakness into a lasting strength?
    (b) Give two examples from present day life to show how a small or "minority" group of people can be stronger than a large group.
17. If you have heard, or heard about, any "revivalist" preachers, describe their way of preaching. What difference, if any, is there between their preaching and that of the prophets of the Old Testament?

Theme Discussion: Judgement

The main theme of the first part of the Book of Amos is God's judgement of the nations. All the Old Testament prophets were very much concerned with this idea of judgement.

THE ISRAELITES' IDEAS ABOUT JUDGEMENT

Writers in the Old Testament thought of "judgement" in two chief ways:

1. They thought of it as the *Law* of God, and especially as the whole system of rules about right and wrong behaviour which the Israelites developed over many centuries. These rules were based on God's law, and were intended to help people to live in accordance with God's will for them. In the AV the word "judgements" in the plural usually has this meaning.

2. They thought of it as the *activity* of God in judging men and nations. This second meaning is the one with which Amos was chiefly concerned.

The idea that God "judges" is very ancient. We find it in the earliest part of the Old Testament: "Shall not the Judge of all the earth do right?" (Gen. 18.25). In those days every human king sat on his throne to give judgement among his people. So it was thought that God, as the King above all nations, was also their Judge. In fact the title "Judge" was sometimes given to a tribal leader. The Book of Judges in the Bible is about leaders and rulers of this kind, rather than about men who gave formal judgements in a court of law. Thus, to speak of God as the Judge, is to say two things about Him: (1) that He acts with *authority* over men; and (2) that He helps and defends those who do His will, and "punishes" those who disobey Him.

During the earlier periods of their history the Israelites believed that many of the visible events in their lives were actually blessings or punishments sent from God. At that time they did not believe in a life after death. Thus it was natural for them to believe that they would experience the results of God's judgement only during their life in this world. For example, after the Israelites at Sinai (Horeb) had refused to wait for God's word, and had made the golden calf and worshipped it, there was an epidemic of some kind: "And the Lord sent a plague upon the people, because they made the calf which Aaron made" (Exod. 32.35). The Israelites believed that the disease was sent by God as a physical punishment for their impatience and disobedience. In the same way, when a group of religious leaders who opposed Moses were swallowed up in an earthquake, this was believed to be a punishment sent from God for their faithlessness (Num. 16.31–35).

Because the Israelites thought that such definite visible happenings were punishments sent from God, it was natural that the prophets should warn them that their disobedience would be punished by "judgement" of this sort—plagues, famines, drought, earthquakes—and also by defeat in battle. They believed that these disasters happened as a direct result of people's disobedience to God. Human beings are part of God's creation. If they refuse to accept God's plan for their lives then they cannot escape from suffering. Amos made it clear that God's law and His judgements do not apply to Israel alone. They apply to all men.

The Israelites, however, were in a special position. God had revealed His nature and His will to this nation in a special way. He had called their rulers to serve Him. He had given them His Law, and had warned them of the suffering which would come to those who refused to accept His authority. The Israelites had accepted the Covenant which the Lord made with them at Sinai. Thus they had bound themselves to serve His holy purpose, and their priests and holy men had taught them how to worship Him and how to behave. It was doubly wrong, therefore, for the Israelites to follow pagan ways and disobey God's laws. They were turning their backs on the great gifts of God. They were also refusing to accept the task and the joy of sharing in God's purpose of saving the world from the power of evil. The prophets saw this clearly, and so they felt compelled to preach the judgement of God upon their own people.

LATER IDEAS ABOUT JUDGEMENT

Later, people came to see that visible sufferings cannot always be called "punishments". Experience shows us that there is not always a direct connection between a person's suffering and his sin. Those who die in an earthquake are not more sinful people than those who survive; good people as well as bad suffer in hospital every day. It is not always "good" tribes or nations who are victorious in war while "bad" nations are defeated. The story of Job helped the Israelites to understand this, for it showed the suffering of a good man who had done his best to obey God, and did not deserve to be punished.

Jesus also taught this. When the Pharisees asked Him a question about the sin which they believed caused a man's blindness, Jesus replied: "It was not that this man sinned or his parents" (John 9.2–3), but because there was a deeper purpose of God to be shown in the healing of his blindness. Jesus rejected the teaching that people who suffer most are the greatest sinners: "There were some present at that very time who told him of the Galileans whose blood Pilate had mingled with their sacrifices. And he answered 'Do you think that these Galileans were worse sinners than all the other Galileans, because they suffered thus? I tell you No; but unless you repent you will all likewise perish'." (Luke 13.1–5.) Suffering can be a kind of discipline and training, which helps people to understand God's plan for the world, and thus to serve Him better.

So the Israelites, who had believed that God's judgements could always be seen in outward events, gradually came to understand that this is not the case. They began to look towards some future day as the time when God's final judgement of people and actions would be declared. At that time, they believed, everyone who had done good in this life without receiving a reward would find a blessing, and those who had done evil and escaped suffering would find a punishment (see Ps. 94.1–15). Towards the end of the Old Testament period, and at the time when the New Testament was being written, many Jews were looking forward to this day of judgement. The early Christians took over this Jewish belief, and at first believed that the day would come in their own lifetime. People of other religions also, for example Hindus and Muslims, have believed that men's actions will be judged after their death or at some time in the future.

WHAT CHRISTIANS BELIEVE ABOUT JUDGEMENT

Today most Christians hold the following ideas about judgement:

(a) We believe that God is the Lord of all men, and that, therefore, His will must be obeyed. If we do our best to obey, we shall

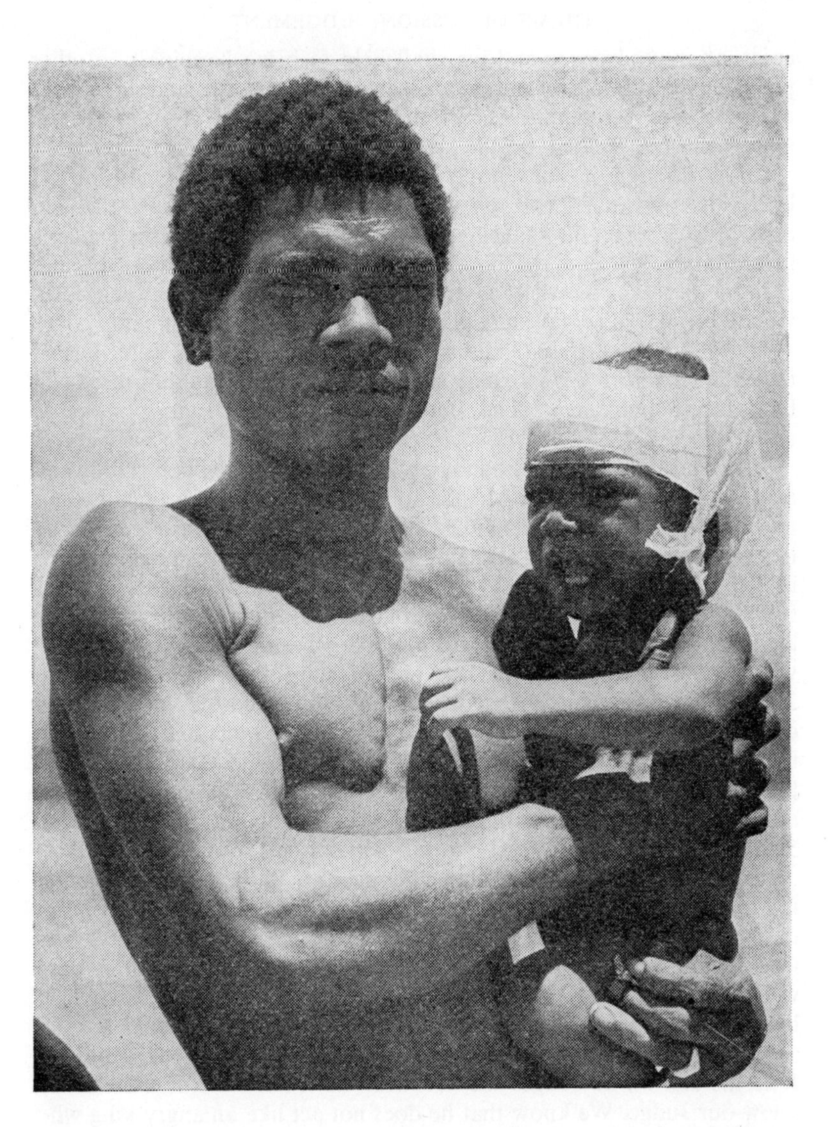

"Visible sufferings cannot always be called 'punishments'. . . there is not always a direct connection between a person's suffering and his sin." (p. 30).

This baby was badly burned during the volcanic eruption of Mount Lamington in New Guinea, which killed nearly 3,000 people.

Whose "sin" caused his suffering?

enjoy an inward peace and we shall help to bring happiness to other people, even though we may not escape from outward suffering. If we disobey, then we cannot expect that the world will grow more and more peaceful, or that people will become more and more happy.

(b) Although it does not seem that every particular sinful act brings its own particular physical punishment, we believe that sin does always result in suffering. If we think of the sin of selfishness, for example, we can see how it leads to wars, class struggles, and racial bitterness, as well as to jealousy and hatred between individual people. We may surely call these results "punishments".

(c) We believe that God's will and purpose will be victorious at the end. Therefore we, too, may share in the expectation that there will be a future judgement. The Book of Revelation certainly supports us in this belief.

(d) The Jews were bound by the Covenant which God had made with them through Moses, and were judged according to their faithfulness to that Covenant. Christians believe themselves to be the people of the *New* Covenant, which God made by sending Jesus into the world, and that they will be judged according to their faithfulness to His teaching. Writing about the Jews, Paul said, "All who have sinned without the law will also perish without the law, and all who have sinned under the law will be judged by the law" (Rom. 2.12). But Jesus taught that His followers would be judged by a different and higher sort of standard: "For if you love those who love you what reward have you? Do not even the tax-collectors do the same? And if you salute only your brethren, what are you doing more than others? Do not even the Gentiles do the same?" (Matt. 5.46–47).

(e) We believe that all human beings are judged by the Son of God: "The Father judges no-one, but has given all judgement to the Son" (John 5.22). Just as in Jesus Christ we see God healing and God suffering, so He is also God judging men. Paul knew this very well. "But with me it is a very small thing that I should be judged by you or by any human court. I do not even judge myself. I am not aware of anything against myself, but I am not thereby acquitted. It is the Lord who judges me" (1 Cor. 4.3–4). If we know Jesus we know our Judge. We know that he does not act like an angry king who enjoys dealing out punishments, but as a loving Father who disciplines His children in order that they may grow in strength and understanding.

(f) Christians rejoice because they know that Jesus came into the world, not chiefly as Judge but as Saviour, in order to save people from the power of evil. Christians belong to this world in which evil is strong. We cannot escape judgement, and because we are measured by the high standard of Jesus Himself we fall short over and over again. Like all human beings we suffer from the results of our sinful actions and as a result of the sins of others. But because Jesus came into the world and Himself suffered punishment for our misdoings, we have been given the sure hope that if we turn to Him God will also forgive us over and over again in spite of our sin. He is a loving and merciful judge as well as a just one. Under this New Covenant, God promises to His sinful people that He will "forgive their iniquity" (Jer. 31.34).

Thus the truth about judgement which Amos preached is important for us as Christians. But we can say more about the result of judgement than he could. "For by grace you have been saved through faith; and this is not your own doing, it is the gift of God" (Eph. 2.8). Amos said, "Seek the Lord and live" (Amos 5.6). We can go on from there and say, "The Lord seeks you and in Christ He died to find you."

STUDY SUGGESTIONS

WORDS

1. Read Psalm 119.73–80. In v. 75 the word "judgements" is used to mean the law of God. List *four* other words used in this passage which have the same meaning as the word "judgements" as it is used in that verse.
2. All of the following words are connected with the idea of judgement as an activity of God. Which of them suggest that the result of the judgement will be (a) punishment, and which suggest that the result will be (b) forgiveness?
   accuse justify acquit condemn convict excuse reprieve absolve testify against reproach pardon

CONTENT

3. (a) What were the two chief ways in which writers in the Old Testament thought of "judgement"?
   (b) With which meaning of the word was Amos particularly concerned?
4. To whom did the Israelites give the title "judge"?
5. "The Israelites believed that many of the visible events in their lives were blessing or punishments sent from God." (p. 29). Give two examples of actual events which the Israelites believed to have been sent by God as a punishment for their sins.
6. "God's law and His judgement . . . apply to all men." (p. 29). Why was it doubly wrong for the Israelites to disobey God's law?

7. Read Job 19.21–29, John 9.2–3, and Luke 13.1–5
   (a) In what way did the story of Job help the Israelites to understand that there is not always a direct connection between a person's suffering and his sin?
   (b) What was the teaching of Jesus about the connection between sin and suffering?
8. Some of the ideas about judgement which Christians hold today are listed on pp. 30, 32. Which of these ideas were also held by the Israelites at the time of Amos?

BIBLE

9. (a) Read Lev. 26.3–7; Lev. 26.14–20; Matt. 19.34, 36; John 8.50, 51. What is the difference between the teaching of Moses and the teaching of Jesus about the results of God's judgement: (i) for the people who obey His commandments; and (ii) for those who fail to keep His commandments?
10. Jesus said: "Judge not, that you be not judged" (Matt. 7.1). Does this mean that a Christian ought not to act as a judge in a court of law? If not, what does it mean?
11. "To speak of God as the Judge is to say two things" (p 29).
    (a) What are those two things?
    (b) Which of them is said in each of the following passages? Gen. 18.25; 1 Sam. 2.10; Ps. 96.10; Isa. 33.22; Ezek. 7.3; 1 Cor. 4.3, 4; Heb. 10.29, 30.

APPLICATION, OPINION, RESEARCH

12. Some Christians believe that there will be a "time for the dead to be judged" (Rev. 11.18) or "hour of his judgement" (Rev. 14.7) at some future date, when God will reward those who have served Him faithfully, and destroy those who have refused to accept His authority. Other Christians believe that judgement came with Jesus and is going on all the time: "*Now* is the judgement" (John 12.31).
    (a) Is it possible to hold both these beliefs at the same time? Give examples in support of your answer.
    (b) What is the teaching of your own Church about judgement?
    (c) Find out, if you can, what beliefs about judgement by God, either during our life on earth or after death, are held by people of other religions in your country.
13. What would you reply to someone who said:
    (a) "There is always a direct connection between a person's suffering and his sin"?
    (b) "Suffering does not come from sin, but from natural causes which scientists can discover and overcome"?

PART II 3.1—4.13
PREACHING TO ISRAEL

INTRODUCTION

Chapters 3 and 4 of the Book of Amos record some of the sayings of the prophet while he was preaching to his people in Israel. These chapters, and also chapters 5 and 6, are made up of short passages rather loosely connected together. For this reason we cannot expect to find a single theme being developed, or a single "sermon plan" being followed. What we can see clearly from these chapters is that Amos was a man with a message. Of course, we can say the same thing about any speaker who tries to persuade his hearers to accept a particular belief or follow a particular course of action. A salesman trying to sell you a tin of meat is a man with a message. A health officer trying to encourage people to get rid of mosquitoes is a man with a message. But Amos was a man with a *divine* message, a word which he claimed had come to him from God. That is why his preaching was so forceful; that is what makes it so valuable. He was speaking 2,800 years ago, yet his words are full of freshness and meaning for us today.

We may imagine Amos, then, in Israel: Perhaps he spoke to the people when they were gathered together near to the holy place of Bethel on its hill, or perhaps in a crowded marketplace of Samaria.

Israel's Responsibility 3.1–15

SUMMARY AND BACKGROUND

The chief subject of this section is the special situation of Israel. Amos tried to convince the Israelites that if they continued to behave as though their covenant with God had never existed, then they would have to suffer the consequences. He believed that the special relationship between God and Israel meant that God had given the Israelites special responsibilities.

INTERPRETATION AND NOTES

3.1. Israel: When Amos used this name he was clearly applying it to the whole people, in both kingdoms, north and south, and not to the inhabitants of the northern kingdom only. He thought of the Israelites as still belonging to one family, though now divided into two groups.

3.2. You only . . . : This is the most important verse of the whole chapter, the key to all that Amos was saying. The phrase: "You only have I known" would be understood by all Israelites as a summary of their special relationship with God. God had spoken to Israel. He had called the people of Israel and cherished them in a unique way. Therefore, most Israelites thought that God would spare them even when they deserved punishment and sorrow. But Amos stated the opposite; "*therefore* I will punish you for all your iniquities." This message came as a painful shock to the Israelites. They had thought that their calling by God meant that their punishment would be lightened. Amos was saying that *because* of their calling, their punishment would be all the more severe.

What did Amos mean when he said, "You only have I known"? It is of course true to say that God knew and knows *all* the peoples of the earth. But the word "to *know,*" as Amos used it in this passage, means more than "to know about". It means "to have a close relationship with", "to be like a husband", "to love" in a special way. And in this sense Israel did stand in a special, unique position. So far as we know, God has not been related in quite the same way to any other nation.

Some people find it difficult to accept that God should choose one nation to be His people in a special way. It seems to them to mean that God has favourites among His children, and that He loves some more than others. They ask, "How can God be just if He is not fair, if He does not give equal chances to all?" This question has caused some thinkers to deny that God made a special Covenant with Israel. We may find it easier to answer if we consider three truths:

1. Every creature, every man, every nation is an individual, unique. No two people are exactly alike. So it is reasonable to expect that one nation will be in advance of the others in its religion, another will be in advance in its art, and so on.
2. If God is active in the world at all, then His actions will be seen in particular places at particular times. For example, if, as we believe, God works to renew and reform the Church, then He will do it through individual men and women in the particular places where they live and work.
3. When God did choose one people, it was not simply to show them His favour. It was in order that they should carry out His purpose for all the nations. We may think of a government deciding to build a new college or a new hospital. Town A may be chosen as the site for it, rather than towns B or C; but the new building is to serve the people of *all* the towns. In the same way, Israel was chosen

to *serve* other nations, not to have mastery and power over them.

3.3–8. The Lord has spoken: We can imagine that after hearing the words recorded in v. 2 the crowd made many objections. They probably asked what right this ignorant countryman Amos had, to speak so sternly to civilized townspeople. Amos answered them by giving a series of brief word-pictures in which he showed that particular events are certain to result from particular causes. Then he showed the "cause" of his own preaching: "The Lord has spoken; who can but prophesy?" (v. 8). This was the way in which Amos defended his words. He had no choice in the matter, since God had spoken to him.

Most of the "word-pictures" in this section are taken from country life, which of course Amos knew well. Jesus used word-pictures of everyday events in this same way when He was speaking to the crowds in Galilee: "When you see a cloud rising in the west, you say at once, 'A shower is coming'; and so it happens." The events He described all had causes which everyone understood. (See Luke 12.54–56.)

3.6. Does evil befall a city, unless the Lord has done it? This phrase shows that Amos, like most people of his time, thought that God's action can constantly be seen in historical events. He believed that it was God Himself who made a city prosperous or caused its defeat in war. Many people still hold this kind of belief: Muslims, for example, are taught that every event, however small and unimportant, is directly willed by God. And so do some Christian people. A fisherman will say, "We have had a bad catch today", or a farmer will say, "Yesterday's storm will have ruined the fruit harvest"—and both will go on to say, "This is God's will, because there were so few people in Church on Sunday", or "because the people in this place are so sinful". But most Christians today would be much more cautious about seeing direct divine action in the events of history or of their daily lives. (See Theme Discussion on Judgement, p. 30.)

3.7. Surely God does nothing without revealing his secret to . . . the prophets: Some scholars think that this verse does not really belong to this passage, as it interrupts the series of questions. But it does provide a sort of introduction to v. 8 by showing clearly what Amos himself believed about prophecy. The prophets were privileged to share in God's plans and to know the causes of His actions. It was their inescapable duty, as His servants, to warn the people of the events which would result from those actions.

3.9–11. Assemble yourselves . . . and see: In this passage Amos was calling on the powerful enemy nations of Assyria and Egypt to come and see the disorder and oppression in Israel. Even pagan nations like these would recognize the wickedness of Samaria. Both were so strong that they could defeat Israel at any time.

"Hear this word that the Lord has spoken . . . 'You only have I known of all the families of the earth; therefore will I punish you' " (Amos 3.2). "Israel was chosen to serve other nations, not to have power over them." (pp. 36, 37)

Mrs Kisosonkole was responsible as Uganda's representative, serving on the Social, Humanitarian, and Cultural Committee of the UN to secure Human Rights for the people of all nations.

In what other ways can individual Christians today serve the people of other nations?

Although in v. 11 Amos spoke simply of "an adversary", and did not actually name Assyria, he probably foresaw the attack which was going to come from that nation. He foresaw that the Israelites would be quickly defeated, because they had broken the Covenant and no longer deserved God's care: "They do not know how to do right" (v. 10). Amos saw that the trouble and discontent within the nation would give Israel's enemies a good opportunity to attack.

3.12. As the shepherd . . . : This verse stands on its own, unconnected with vv. 11 or 13. The editor probably placed it here because it describes the results of the attack which Amos had foreseen (v. 11), and so can be read as a proof that Amos's prophecy was fulfilled. Amos was speaking from his own experience as a shepherd, when he compared what would be left of Israel by her attackers, with the scraps of skin and bone left by a lion that has attacked a sheep.

It is interesting to note how often lions are mentioned in the Old Testament. Today there are no wild animals of that size left in the whole of the Near East. Vegetation has changed, and probably the climate has changed as a result. The forests were cut down, the land became more and more sandy, and less rain fell. The country is now too thinly covered in bush, and too thickly inhabited, to support such wild life.

3.13–15. Altars of Bethel: These were the holiest place in the northern kingdom. They were used as a place of worship by the royal family (see the notes on 7.13). The "horns of the altar" were rather like handles which stuck out from the four corners. It was the tradition in Israel that if a criminal could run to the altar in a temple sanctuary, and put his hand on one of these horns, then he was safe and must not be ill-treated. There is a very vivid story about this custom in 1 Kings 2.28–35. In English the word "sanctuary" (which comes from the Latin *sanctus,* "holy") means both a holy place, and a place where people are safe from harm. If a place is kept holy because it has been dedicated to the worship of God, then people regard that place and everything in it as being protected by the Lord. But Amos foresaw that even the "horns of the altar" would be destroyed (v. 14). He could see no safe place in Israel.

3.13. The house of Jacob: Another way of referring to Israel, by using the name of an ancestor from whom the people were descended. The "house" means the clan or family of Jacob.

3.15. The winter house ... the summer house: It seems that some of the rich people in Samaria built very expensive homes, suitable for both hot and cold weather. But the phrase is not clear; it may mean two separate houses, or two separate parts of one large building. Today in hot countries rich people often have a summer house in the hills where they can escape the worst of the heat.

Houses of ivory; This does not mean built out of ivory, but decorated with it. Amos prophesied that all these rich houses would be destroyed, as indeed they were when the Assyrians came.

STUDY SUGGESTIONS

WORDS

1. "You only have I known" (Amos 3.2b). In which of the following sentences does the word "know" have the same meaning as it has in this verse?
   (a) Do you know the difference between good and evil?
   (b) He knows that his sister has arrived.
   (c) I have many friends, but I know my parents best of all.
   (d) That man knows how to play football.

CONTENT

2. "A salesman trying to sell you a tin of meat is a man with a message" (p. 35)—and so is a health officer trying to encourage people to get rid of mosquitoes.
   (a) In what chief ways is the message of a health officer different from that of a meat salesman?
   (b) In what chief ways was the message of the prophets of Israel different from either?
3. What is the chief subject of Amos's message in 3.1–15?
4. What or whom did Amos mean by:
   (a) "people of Israel" (3.1)?
   (b) "an adversary" (3.11)?
   (c) "the house of Jacob" (3.13)?
   (d) "the altars of Bethel" (3.14)?
   (e) "the winter house" and "the summer house" (3.15)?
5. "When God did choose one people, it was not simply to show them His favour." (p. 36).
   What did He choose them for?

BIBLE

6. Read 1 Kings 1.49–53; 1 Kings 2.28–35; Ps. 20.1, 2.
   (a) The word "sanctuary" can mean two different sorts of place. What are they?
   (b) Give examples of places which are regarded as "sanctuaries" today.
   (c) By whom and for what reasons are they regarded as sanctuaries?
7. In the following passages we read of people who all had the same sort of feeling or experience.
   (i) What was the experience?

(ii) Name the person in each case who had the experience.
(a) Isa. 61.1–3; (b) Amos 3.8b; (c) Gal. 1.11–12.

8. Read Isa. 28.24, 25; Matt. 16.2, 3; Jas. 3.10–12. In what way are these passages like Amos 3.3–6?

APPLICATION, OPINION, RESEARCH

9. We have seen that the prophets felt they had received a message from God.
   (a) What sort of people today, if any, claim to have received such a message, and what reasons do they give for this claim?
   (b) Do you think that their claims are true? Give reasons for your answer.
   (c) In what ways can people best pass on such a message today?
10. "Some people find it difficult to accept that God should choose one nation to be His people in a special way." (p. 36)
    What is your opinion?
11. "Most Christians today would be cautious about seeing direct divine action in . . . events."
    (a) What does your Church teach about this?
    (b) What is your own opinion?
    Give examples from everyday life to support your answer.

2. The need for social and religious honesty 4.1–13

SUMMARY AND BACKGROUND

Chapter 4 contains further selections from the sayings of Amos. Four separate short passages seem to have been brought together. Vv. 1–3 contain a very strong attack on the rich people of Samaria. Vv. 4 and 5 contain ironic and sarcastic words showing up the dishonesty and hypocrisy of the worship in the Israelite holy places. Vv. 6–12 contain a reminder of warnings which God had already given to Israel. In each case the people had ignored the warning. Now they must prepare to suffer the results of their stubbornness (v. 12). V. 13 is a short hymn of praise for the power and glory of God who will deal with these disobedient people.

INTERPRETATION AND NOTES

4.13. You cows of Bashan: The words which Amos used were not at all polite. This was an insulting way to speak to the wealthy

"Hear this word, you . . . who oppress the poor . . . the days are coming upon you, when . . . you shall be cast forth" (Amos 4.1, 2, 3).

Marchers in China support revolution against "imperialists" who are said to exploit the people of underdeveloped nations. In India political parties spend millions of pounds on election campaigns, hoping to "cast forth" their opponents.

But perhaps the matter is not so simple. What real hope do either the banners or the posters offer to a man who lies starving in the street?

women of Samaria. Bashan was good farming country east of the sea of Galilee, known for its fine fat cattle. Amos saw that these Samaritan women were fat and lazy, lovers of luxury, and unfair to the poor.

It is not very clear from the Hebrew what punishment they were to suffer (vv. 2 and 3), but we can understand the general meaning. The walls of the city will be broken down. The rich women will be killed, and their bodies will be dragged through the gaps in the walls to lie rotting outside. It is not known whether the word "Harmon" is the name of a place or has some other meaning. In the RSV it is left in Hebrew; in the AV it is translated as "the palace"; and other scholars have suggested that it might mean "in nakedness" or "to the refuse heap". When the scholars' opinions are so varied, it seems best to say that we do not know the meaning.

In this passage we can surely see some of the feelings of the man from the country when he meets city life. Amos came from a hard life as a farmer in Judah. In the country, poverty is shared by all when the harvest is poor. But in the town Amos saw extremes of wealth and poverty side by side.To him this showed Israel's neglect of God. It is interesting to note how often country people feel like this when they meet city life. "If you go to Suva, or Port Moresby—or Nairobi or Lagos or Calcutta, or whatever the big city may be—then you will see all the wickedness of life." This is a common feeling, and there is surely some truth in it. In a city the individual is lost in a crowd. The influence of family or tribe is not so strong as it is in the country, so that a person can easily follow ways of living that his parents or teachers disapprove of. But of course this is not the whole truth. There are sins in country life, and there are honest and generous people in cities.

4.4, 5. Come ... and transgress: In this passage Amos was using sarcasm in order to denounce the falseness of religious life in Israel. "Come on," he said, "Increase your offerings and sacrifices, make as much public noise about your gifts as you can!" If Amos were living today he might say that to make a public show of one's religion is "transgression", for it is against the purpose of God. In 2.7–8 Amos had denounced the people's conduct at the holy places. To increase that sort of "religious" behaviour would be to increase in sin. Although the evils in Jewish worship were not so obvious in New Testament times, Jesus was giving a similar kind of warning when He said: "When you give alms sound no trumpet before you, as the hypocrites do in the synagogues and in the streets, that they may be praised by men . . . they love to stand and pray in the synagogues and at the street corners, that they may be seen by men." (Matt. 6.2–6. See also note on Amos 5.21–24.)

4.6–11. You did not return. Amos declared that God had repeatedly warned Israel in the past, by allowing some disaster to happen, and he reminded the people of five of these disasters. In each case, the event had been God's way of showing the people their folly, but in each case they had ignored His warning. So after describing each event, Amos repeated the phrase: "Yet you did not return to me, says the Lord." Another example of warnings from God of which we read in the Bible is the series of plagues on Egypt described in Exodus 7—11. The words "after the manner of Egypt" (v. 10) seem to show that Amos had this in mind. There is also some likeness to the terrible series of warnings in Deuteronomy 28.15–57: "All these curses shall come upon you . . . because you did not obey the voice of the Lord your God."

The warnings of which Amos reminded the Israelites were:

1. *A famine* (v. 6). The phrase "cleanness of teeth" was his vivid way of describing hunger.

2. *A drought* (vv. 7, 8). As this had come "when there were yet three months to the harvest", it must have meant the loss of the crop, also leading to famine, as well as a shortage of drinking water.

3. *A disease of crops* and *a plague of locusts* (*v.* 9). Amos did not say whether the events described in this verse had all happened at the same time. His experience as a farmer made it natural for him to regard the coming of locusts as a specially severe warning. (See also 7.1–3, and p. 77 below).

4. *An epidemic* of sickness (v. 10). "After the manner of Egypt" may mean that it was like the plague of boils which the Egyptians suffered at the time of Moses and Aaron (Exod. 9.8–12), or it may mean some other form of sickness which had become known as the Egyptian sickness. The phrase about "your horses" is not clear in Hebrew, but the second half of this verse suggests that the epidemic had broken out among the army of Israel rather than among the townspeople.

5. *An earthquake* (v. 11). This may have been the same disaster referred to in 1.1. It must have been a violent one to have been compared to the end of Sodom and Gomorrah. "A brand plucked from the burning" means like a stick snatched out of the fire when everything else is going up in flames.

We should notice that all these disasters mentioned by Amos were *natural* events. They were not the direct result of human action, like a war. There must have been very many people who experienced these events and suffered from them, but evidently most people failed to see them as a warning from God. It was the prophet's gift to be able to interpret such events in terms of the word of God (see also the note on visions, p. 74).

4.12. Thus I will do to you: The actual words of Amos seem to have been abbreviated by the editors, but it is clear that he was warning the Israelites that a worse disaster was to come upon them. The people had chosen to ignore God's repeated warnings, *therefore* they must expect to suffer when God would come to judge them. Amos did not say exactly what form this "judgement", or "meeting" with God, would take. But he showed quite clearly *why* it would take place.

Prepare to meet your God: This phrase has become a favourite motto for "adventists", that is to say, people who expect Jesus to return soon. But even if we do not use the phrase in that way it still has truth for us. To meet God is the end, the climax, the crown of life. It may be a meeting of joy and glory, or it may be one of terror and pain. We are all preparing in one way or another to meet our Lord, but we easily forget this.

4.13. The Lord ... is his name: Some scholars think that this verse was written by the editor of the book and not by Amos himself, because the language is so different from that of Amos's preaching. There are other verses in the book like this one: e.g. 5.8–9 and 9.5–6. They are what are known as "doxologies", i.e. short songs in praise of God. The purpose of this verse, 4.13, is to remind readers of the nature of God who was dealing with Israel. He is not the god of one tribe, or the god of one holy place; he is not a god who can be defeated. He is "the Lord, the God of hosts," the creator of the universe. The language of this verse is similar to that of Isaiah 40.

STUDY SUGGESTIONS

WORDS

1. What is a "doxology"?

CONTENT

2. (a) Whom did Amos call "cows of Bashan" (4.1)?
   (b) Why did he use this name for them?
   (c) Of what did he accuse them?
3. What is meant by "cleanness of teeth" (4.6)?
4. "God had repeatedly warned Israel ... by allowing some disaster to happen."
   (a) Amos reminded the people of five of these disasters: what were they?
   (b) What had been the Israelites' response to God's warnings?

BIBLE

5. " 'You cows of Bashan' . . . was an insulting way to speak." Read the following passages and say in each case:
   (i) Who was speaking in an insulting way;
   (ii) To whom he was speaking;

(iii) For what reason he was using insulting language.
(a) Matt. 3.4–10; (b) Matt. 23.1–4 and 27, 28; (c) Gal. 3.1–3.

6. (a) Which verses in Amos 4 contain a similar sort of warning to that given in the following passages? Ps. 78.35–37; Matt. 15.7–9; Col. 2.20–23.
   (b) What kind of language did Amos use in order to give this warning?
7. (a) In what ways is v. 13 *different* from the rest of Amos 4?
   (b) In what ways is v. 13 *like* the following? Ps. 65.5–8; Ps. 135.5–7; Isa. 40.12; Jer. 10.12, 13.

APPLICATION, OPINION, RESEARCH

8. (a) What are the chief differences between life in the country or in the bush, and life in a large town or city?
   (b) Some people say that obedience to God is more difficult for people who live in a city. What is your opinion?
   (c) Give examples of opportunities for Christian witness which are open to city dwellers and not to those who live in the country.
9. The Israelites had chosen to ignore God's warnings.
   (a) Give 3 reasons why people are often slow to accept warnings.
   (b) Describe any event in your own life which seemed to you to be a warning.
10. "Amos was using sarcasm in order to denounce the falseness of religious life in Israel." (p. 43).
    Rewrite 4.4, 5 in your own words, using examples of any present-day "religious" behaviour which seems to you to be "false" and "against the purpose of God".
11. A fisherman who had taken only a very poor catch of fish gave many different reasons for his failure:
    his net was torn; the moon was too bright; he had the wrong sort of bait; he had a headache; God was angry because he had not been to Church on Sunday.
    (a) Do you think *all* these reasons could be true? Give reasons for your answer.
    (b) Do you think that God speaks to us through natural events, such as a good or bad harvest, a storm, etc.? If there are messages from God in such things, how can we find the message?
12. Amos 4.13; 5.8, 9; and 9.5, 6 are all "songs of praise" about God the Creator.
    (a) How often is praise of this sort expressed in the public worship of your Church?

(b) Select 3 hymns from the hymnal used in your Church which praise God in the same way as these 3 passages in the Book of Amos.

Theme Discussion: The Christian Contribution to Social Justice

See 2.6, 4.1–3, 5.10,11, 6.4–7

WHAT DO WE MEAN BY "SOCIAL JUSTICE"?

Amos saw in Israel a particular situation in which people had to live, and he did not hesitate to point out the injustice which he saw there. He was deeply concerned about it. He felt that the word of God which he had to speak was not only about false worship, but also about this lack of justice in Israel.

In speaking like this Amos was not doing something altogether new. If we read the Pentateuch we find again and again that the law of God has to do with justice between men. "If there is among you a poor man ... you shall ... lend him sufficient for his need" (see Deut. 15.7–11). "If a Hebrew man is sold to you, in the seventh year you shall let him go free" (see Deut. 15, 12–18). "You shall not oppress a hired servant" (see Deut. 24.14, 15).

The law which God gave to His people in the Old Covenant showed how He intended that men should treat each other. It showed that God intended that there should be justice in society. The holy men and prophets of Israel were all aware of this. For a later example, see 1 Kings 21, where Elijah's word to Ahab was basically a condemnation of his injustice. The king had great power, but he used this royal power to murder and to steal.

We can trace the origin of this "social concern", as we should call it today, in the Old Covenant, right back to the stories about the creation. The early writers declared that God made man "in His own image". If "man" means "mankind in general", then it also means every human being in particular. Every human being is a child of God. The Israelites had to learn that each individual person is equally important, and for that reason no person must be despised or oppressed by his neighbours. God's concern for the poor and starving, for widows and fatherless children, was the pattern which He intended the Israelites to follow. Amos saw that, on the contrary, they had forgotten all this vital part of the Covenant.

When we read the New Testament, we find that this same concern for justice between people was made visible by Jesus in His ministry.

And in the early Church, the Holy Spirit led the apostles to express this same concern in action. "As many as were possessors of lands or houses sold them, and brought the proceeds ... and laid it at the apostles' feet, and distribution was made to each as any had need." (See Acts 4.32–37.)

The phrase "social justice" is often used today to describe the use of power or authority to uphold what is right. For example, a man who owns a factory or manages an estate has power over his workmen, just as in ancient times a master had power over his servants or slaves. If the factory-owner or estate-manager uses that power to keep the workmen poor while he gets rich, or to impose harsh conditions which turn the workmen into frightened slaves, that is social *in*justice. We see social justice if an employer uses his power in such a way as to give his workmen decent conditions of work, a fair reward for their labour, and hope of advancement if the factory or estate prospers. Of course, the workmen, too, have some power. They can fight the employer by working badly, or by refusing to obey him. They can perhaps leave his service; but this may be impossible in a situation where there is no other work available by which they can earn their living. Their power too can be used for justice or injustice, to uphold what is right, or to weaken what is right. Social justice is obviously not a simple matter. It concerns the various sorts of power that men have over one another, and it also concerns people's understanding of what is right.

DIFFICULTIES AND DANGERS

Christians believe that they learn what is right from the revelation of God's will in the Bible, and from the continuing work of the Holy Spirit in their hearts. Yet Christians live in many different situations in many different countries, so it is not surprising that they do not all hold the same opinions about particular kinds of social justice. Through the centuries individual Christians and Churches in different lands have upheld different forms of political organization as the best way to support social justice in their own situation. But from the very beginning of the Church in New Testament times, Christians have always agreed that their faith should be made visible in just relationships between human beings. This has always been an important aim of Christian teaching. In practice there have been many obstacles and temptations which have prevented people from achieving that aim. Some of these difficulties are:

1. Christian people may be so concerned about their relationship with God that they forget their relationship with their fellow men.

This lack of balance may arise from a genuine desire to make the Church a holy fellowship. It may lead to beautiful services of worship, to real self-examination, and to frequent prayer. But it can also lead us to shirk our responsibility for the good ordering of the community in which we live. It can lead to carelessness about the way our country is governed, and to a selfish neglect of the needs of people who are poorer or less well educated than ourselves.

2. At certain places and times in history the Church has been very closely linked to the government of a city or nation.

Sometimes, if the friendship between Church and government is close, then the Church will not want to criticize the government, for it will not want to lose its position and power in the nation. When that happens the voice of the Church may be silenced. For example, during the last thirty years the Roman Catholic Church in Spain has been very close to the government of that country. Perhaps as a result of this, the Church in Spain has not spoken at all clearly when the government there has persecuted its political opponents. Similarly in South Africa the Dutch Reformed Church, in its teaching and its structure, is closely allied to the government and so encourages its racial policies. On a much smaller scale, the Churches in the island of Samoa and Tonga have been so closely linked with the system of rule by chiefs that they have not yet done much serious questioning about the right place of chiefs in society, or the power which the chiefs ought to have over the people.

3. Another danger arises when the Church makes gifts to the poor, but does not take the trouble to seek out the cause of their poverty, or try to correct that cause.

In places where there are beggars on the streets, Christians may feel that it is their duty to give them small coins. But this action by itself does nothing to answer the root questions—what made the man into a beggar in the first place, and how can his condition of life be improved? It does nothing to prevent future generations from having to beg for a living instead of leading useful and satisfying lives. "Charity", or the giving of presents, can thus become an unsatisfactory alternative to social action.

4. A further danger is for the Church to take action about social problems without a proper understanding of the situation. This may happen when people apply a particular doctrine without really thinking about it. Or it may happen when sudden bursts of enthusiasm drive people to act before they understand what the results of their action may be.

Something like this appears to have happened regarding polygamy in parts of Africa, and elsewhere, especially in the late nineteenth century. Much of the teaching in the New Testament shows that men and women can serve God, and each other, better in a monogamous marriage than in a polygamous one. And where polygamy is the custom, women usually have a very low status in society. For these reasons most Christian missionaries believed that to abolish polygamy in these countries was an important step towards a better way of life. Yet to abolish the custom all at once created many problems, and in some cases actually increased injustice. The separated wives might have no opportunity of remarrying, and others had no way of earning a living for themselves and their children. Unless the whole way of living of the tribe was changed, the sudden abolition of this one custom could and did bring much unhappiness for a time. Enthusiasm cannot take the place of study and understanding.

With all these dangers it is not surprising that the Church has often failed to put its faith into practice in the area of social justice. It seems that today most Churches do give a very important place in their teaching to this branch of practical Christianity. In many countries the attitude of the Church to social and political questions is partly due to the lessons which Christians have learned from the communist revolutionaries. These have shown whole nations overturned in an effort to establish a way of life which will be equally fair for all citizens. The revolutionary leaders have aimed at giving people freedom from poverty, from oppression by harsh landlords and employers, and from the fear of unemployment. In doing so, they have denied people other freedoms which Christians believe to be even more important, and for this reason many Christians think that they have been mistaken, and have created more injustice than they have cured. But from the practical effort of communists to reform society from its very roots, the Church has learnt the *power* that there is in man's struggle to get justice.

CHRISTIAN RESPONSIBILITY AND SOCIAL JUSTICE

It is plain that the teaching of Amos, with his concern about the rich and the poor, is of great importance for us today. He reminds us that the struggle to make a just society is a *religious* matter. We must, of course, recognize that very many of the people who work for social justice are not Christians. In many nations of the world people of other religions, and people who would not call themselves religious at all, are working in their personal lives, or through such bodies as the various United Nations agencies, to create better lives for their fellow-countrymen. But as the Church co-operates with others it is important to remember the *special* reasons why Christians should be active in that work, and the special truths they need to remember in doing so:

1. Christians take part in social action because they love and honour God. They desire to see His will done on earth as it is in heaven. And they believe it to be His will that every human being should have

“In many nations people who would not call themselves religious at all are working to create better lives for their fellow-countrymen . . . But evil is not wiped out when we have improved the conditions in which poor people have to live.” (p. 53).

The crime-rate among young people in this new block of flats in Paris, France, is the highest in the whole city.

What more do the poor need, besides better material conditions?

an equal right to enjoy the gifts and use the talents which He has provided. So we must be careful not to base our action on jealousy of people who are richer than we are, or on pride in our race, or on hatred of foreigners or immigrants. In other words, our concern for social action grows out of our faith in God as Father and Lord. Jesus pointed out just how closely these two aspects of faith are bound together: "Truly I say to you, as you did it to one of the least of these my brethren, you did it to me" (Matt. 25.40).

2. The conscience of each individual Christian, and the conscience of the whole Church, are enlightened by the Holy Spirit (John 14.26). So we might expect the Church to be the first part of the nation to see injustice, to expose it, to try to heal it. But sadly we have to confess that this is often not the case. Only too often individual Christians close their ears to the voice of conscience, and the Church has frequently closed its eyes to social problems. For example, in the Pacific islands, as in many parts of the world, there has been a great movement of people from the country villages to the towns. In the Pacific this nearly always creates difficult problems of justice regarding land rights. Land is usually held by a family or tribe and not by individuals, and the family or tribe has no right to sell its land to anyone else. So a villager coming to a town finds it very difficult to get a home. Is he to become a squatter on other people's land, with no rights at all? Or will he be chased off the land? Or should some land be taken from the owners so that he can rent a little piece for himself? Most of the Churches have been slow to recognize this problem. In some places they have helped to establish low-cost housing-schemes, but these efforts are too little, and perhaps too late. In some other areas of life Christians have been among the first to take action in order to solve social problems, for example the World Council of Churches Refugee Service, and we can be thankful for such enterprise.

3. Jesus taught that citizens should respect the laws of their country (see Mark 12.17), and so did the apostles (see Rom. 13.1–3; 1 Pet. 2.13–14). So even when Christians think that a certain law is a bad one, it seems that they should disobey it only if there is no chance at all of changing it. Disobeying a law is one extreme method of taking social action, and Christians have to be ready to pay the penalty for doing so. The early Christians in Rome disobeyed the law about worshipping Caesar—for they could not change the law—even though the penalty for disobedience was death. Christians in some communist and other totalitarian countries today may be faced with this sort of testing situation.

4. The words and work of Jesus show us that God loves and values every individual human being. Thus Christians are called to serve individual people whom they know, and not just "society" as a

whole. St Paul sets an example in his letter to Philemon. He was clearly more determined to put right the personal relationship between Philemon and Onesimus than to attack the custom of slavery itself. In the same way, a Christian pastor may be called to undertake the slow work of helping men and women in prison to become more useful citizens, or helping individual immigrants to find accommodation. Such personal work is just as important in creating social justice as joining an action committee or speaking at political meetings, and it is often more difficult.

5. Christians also need to remember that the better form of human society which they hope to build is not the same thing as the Kingdom of God. We do have this immediate job to do in the world around us. But that is not the end of the road for us. Evil is not wiped out when we have improved the conditions in which poor people have to live. It is God alone who is finally in control of His creation, and who will re-make it according to His purpose. All our attempts to get justice are partial and temporary; they are not final. They are a part we can take in the total purpose of God for human society, but we must be careful not to regard them as the *only* way of carrying out His will in the world.

STUDY SUGGESTIONS

WORDS

1. Which *four* of the following words are nearest in meaning to the word "social" as it is used in this discussion?
   festive public popular sociable communal communist fashionable official
2. Which *four* of the following words are nearest in meaning to the word "justice" as it is used in this discussion?
   judgement equality fairness exactitude righteousness accuracy order love

BIBLE

3. (a) Read Deut. 15.7–11; Deut. 24.14, 15; Isa. 3.13–15; Jer. 22.13–17 and Amos 2.6. In your own words, summarize briefly the teaching about social justice given in these passages by Moses and the three later prophets.
   (b) Read Matt. 25.32–46; Mark 10.23–25; Luke 6.20–25 and Luke 10.29–37. In your own words summarize briefly the teaching of Jesus about social justice.
   (c) What differences, if any, are there between the prophets' teaching and the teaching of Jesus on this subject?

APPLICATION, OPINION, RESEARCH

4. "Christians have always agreed that their faith should be made visible in just relationships between human beings" (p. 48).
   (a) What four difficulties which prevent people from making their faith visible are discussed in the chapter?
   (b) What other difficulties which prevented just relationships between human beings have you seen or experienced in your own country or Church, or in your own life?
   (c) What practical steps can a particular Church or congregation take, in order to overcome these difficulties?
5. "Social justice concerns the various sorts of power that men have over one another." (p. 48).
   (a) Give examples of power which men have over one another in your own country, which might lead to injustice.
   (b) Look through a recent newspaper, and see how many of the incidents reported are concerned with injustice between human beings.
6. (a) A student in New Guinea asked: "Is it right for a Christian to pay taxes if he believes the Government is acting in an unjust way?"
   What is your opinion? Give reasons.
   (b) Read Rom. 13.1–3 and 1 Pet. 2.13, 14.
      (i) In what circumstances, if any, do you think a Christian should disobey the law of the country?
      (ii) What, if anything, can an individual Christian do in order to change a law that is unjust?
7. "Many of the people who work for social justice are not Christians".
   (a) What special organizations do you know of that are working to relieve poverty and ignorance?
   (b) How many of them are related to the Church?
   (c) What if anything have Christians to learn from those that are not related to the Church?
8. (a) What would you reply to someone who said, "The struggle to make a just society is *not* a religious matter. The Church has no business to interfere in the government's plans for housing, welfare, education, etc."?
   (b) Give three special reasons why Christians should work for social justice.
9. Do you think it is right that some people should have better homes, or more land, or a better education than others? Give reasons for your answer.

PART III 5.1—6.14
TRUE AND FALSE RELIGION

INTRODUCTION

The chief theme in chapters 5 and 6 is the contrast between true religion and false religion, between the hope and the despair that they bring to Israel. This part of the book shows clearly that Amos's chief message was unhopeful. He spoke repeatedly about the falseness of the Israelites' religion, and about the punishment which God would bring on His people. Amos was not like the preachers condemned by Jeremiah, who "have healed the wound of my people lightly, saying 'Peace, peace', when there is no peace" (Jer. 6.14). Amos spoke of war, in which Israel's wound would be a death wound.

In spite of this, however, we find in this section that Amos had *some* hope that his preaching might have a good effect: "Seek the Lord and live" (Amos 5.6); "It may be that the Lord . . . will be gracious" (5.15). No man could preach as Amos did without hoping that some of those who heard him would turn away from evil. Was he successful? He did not succeed in turning the nation of Israel from its "transgression". The "punishment" of Israel was not "revoked" (see 1.6 etc.; 2.1 etc.). But the very fact that the message of Amos has been preserved for us shows that some people listened and remembered. There were some who honoured the prophet and his message, and who gave service to God. From these chapters we see that Amos was preaching with the aim of changing the minds of his hearers, as many Christian preachers do today.

1. The Choice Confronting Israel 5.1–17

SUMMARY AND BACKGROUND

The "editors" who put together the Book of Amos divided his sayings into chapters or sections as a help to readers. But the divisions are not very clear in the words themselves. These seventeen verses are a collection of short sayings, not a single message spoken at one time. They contain: a funeral song (vv. 1–3); a call to repent (vv. 4–7); part of a song of praise (vv. 8–9); a warning about injustice (vv. 10–13); a further call to repent (vv. 14–15); and a further funeral song, or vision of death (vv. 16–17).

Verses 8 and 9 contain the same ideas as 4.13, about the greatness of God the Creator. The editor of the book may have included them at this point to show how Amos had contrasted the holiness of God with the sinfulness of Israel's leaders who had "cast down righteousness" (see note on v. 7).

INTERPRETATION AND NOTES

5.1–3. This word ... in lamentation: It was the custom in Israel, as it is in many countries today, for mourners at a funeral to sing about the person who had died. So Amos told his hearers what he would sing about Israel's destruction.
5.2. The virgin Israel; forsaken on her land: was the nation which God had chosen as a man chooses his bride. But like a bride who breaks her engagement, Israel would be left without a protector. Amos foresaw that Israel would lose ninety per cent of its army in the war which was to come. It would be a total war with no mercy from the invader.
5.4–7. Seek me ... do not seek Bethel: These are clear words of challenge to the people. Amos showed plainly the choice which they must face. *Either* they could continue to worship at the "holy places" and join in the pagan activity which went on there (see notes on 2.7–8 and 4.4 5, above), *or* they could "seek the Lord and live". As we have already seen, **Bethel** and **Gilgal** were the most important places of worship in the northern kingdom. **Beersheba** was in the far south of Judah, and was a holy place connected with the stories of Isaac.
5.5. Cross over: By this Amos meant "to go from the north to the south". Many of the Israelites thought that simply by going to these places and making sacrifices there they would be pleasing God. Amos denied this. For Amos, to "seek the Lord" meant (a) living one's whole life in accordance with God's law (5.14), and (b) offering Him the "spiritual" worship of praise and obedience (5.21–23).

Amos used the word "live" (vv. 4 and 6) to describe the alternative to destruction which God was still offering to His people. He was probably thinking of two different sorts of "life":

1. Christians believe that death is a doorway which leads to a new sort of life. But the people of Israel had no such belief in life after death. In their minds death was associated with the punishment of sin: "You are dust and to dust you shall return" (Gen. 3.19). They feared death because they believed that it cut off men from all relationship with God. "I am ... like the slain that lie in the grave, like those whom thou dost remember no more, for they are cut off from thy hand" (Ps. 88.4, 5). They thought that after death men became

"Seek good, and not evil, that you may live" (Amos 5.14). "Amos spoke of war, in which Israel's wound would be a death wound . . . Some people listened and remembered." (p. 55).

Housewives in San Francisco seek to change their government's policy about using the cruelties of war to settle disputes with other nations. They want to save the lives of *all* children, the enemy's as well as their own.

Are they being "unpatriotic" by behaving in this way?

shadows with no real life in them, so death would be the end of all that was good in life.

Amos foresaw that death was coming to Israel. So when he said "Seek the Lord and live", he may have meant that by changing their ways and seeking God truly, the Israelites might escape from being killed by their enemies, rather as Noah was saved from the flood.

2. But Amos may also have been using the word to mean more than "life" simply as the opposite of physical death. Amos saw that the best and fullest sort of life is life in obedience to the will of God. The life which he saw in Israel was not life as it ought to be and could be. So Amos urged the people to "seek the Lord", and thus to live more fully, as His children.

5.6. Break out like fire: As we have seen (p. 18), Amos continually used the idea of fire to describe destruction in war. So he was saying that the idols which people worshipped at Bethel had no power to "quench" the fire that God would send as a punishment on the "house" or descendants of Joseph, i.e. the people of Israel (see note on 3.13, p. 39).

Verse 7 seems incomplete in the Hebrew, and some scholars think that it should be connected with verse 10 (see NEB). Amos may have been directly accusing his hearers of "turning justice to wormwood" (wormwood is a plant with a very bitter flavour whose name came to be used for bitterness), as the RSV and NEB translations suggest. Or he may have been saying "woe" to those who did so. In either case his meaning is clear enough.

5.8. The Pleiades and Orion are groups of stars. Amos was reminding his hearers that God whom they had disobeyed is Creator of the universe, with power over the whole of nature. In the phrase "the Lord is his name" he was reminding the Israelites that the Creator of the earth was well known to them. He was not an unknown God, He was the same Lord who had made the Covenant with their ancestors. (See note on 4.13.)

5.10–13. In the gate: In this passage Amos was accusing Israel's leaders of injustice.

Every town and village has its regular "meeting place", where the chief citizens or "elders", or elected representatives of the people, come together to discuss the affairs of the community. In a large town or city it may be the Council Chamber or the Parliament House or the Law Court—or a trade union office or business men's club. In a village it may be the chief man's house, or an open square—or perhaps simply the shade of a particular tree. This is the place where disputes are settled and practical decisions are made that will lead to justice—or to injustice. In Israel the city gates were the place where people met for discussion and the elders sat as a town council.

Amos believed that the city gate should be the place where people could expect their cases to be judged fairly. But he saw that the elders of Israel were unjust and corrupt. They took bribes (v. 12), and grew rich from the heavy fines: "exactions of wheat" (v. 11), which they imposed. They hated anyone who could not be persuaded to give false witness in a case, or who was brave enough to speak the truth about their unjust behaviour (v. 10). They refused even to hear the cases of "the needy" (v. 12) who could not afford to offer bribes, though it was their duty to do so without payment.

5.11. Houses of hewn stone ... vineyards: Most of the Israelites could only afford houses made of sun-baked clay. The stone houses and large vineyards of the leaders showed that they were enriching themselves at the expense of the poor. But the prophet saw that the rich people had little time remaining in which to enjoy their houses and lands. This warning which Amos gave to the Israelites was very much like the warning which Jesus gave in the parable about a man who put all his trust in riches (Luke 12.16–21).

5.13. The **prudent** man is one who thinks carefully about his actions and makes sure that he will not suffer for what he does. Such a man would have kept silent before the elders of Israel. He would not have taken the risk of speaking out. Amos was not a prudent man. He could not "keep silent in such a time", but felt compelled to speak (3.8).

5.14, 15: These verses seem to be a continuation of the challenge contained in vv. 4–6. They show a little more of what Amos meant by "seeking the Lord". If people want to come closer to God they must "seek good" and "love good". The Old Covenant had revealed this truth to Israel. In the law, God had made it clear that what a man *does* is closely connected with what he *believes*. This may be summarized in the phrase, "You shall be holy, for I the Lord your God am holy" (Lev. 19.2). Amos realized that there was no other way in which the Israelites—or anyone else—could "seek God", except by rejecting their evil ways of life and worship.

5.15. The remnant of Joseph would be the small number of Israelites left alive after the destruction to come. Amos saw no hope for the nation as a whole, but he thought it possible that God would spare a few.

This reminds us of an important truth about the way God works in the world. As we study the Old Testament we find that there were many occasions when a whole nation deserve to die. But on each occasion God in His mercy preserved a few through whom He would continue to carry out His purpose for the World. We see this first in the story of Noah, when God spared a few who were faithful from the flood which destroyed all others. Many of the prophets, especially Isaiah, Jeremiah, and Ezekiel, understood that God works in this way through a "remnant". Each in his time saw that the majority of God's people were faithless, but that there were a few who kept alive the true faith. Only a few went through the experience of captivity in Babylon without losing their faith, but these were the remnant which was to be the hope of Israel, and the preparation for the coming of the Messiah.

5.16, 17: This is another passage in which Amos expressed his belief that great sorrow was coming to Israel.

5.16. The squares were the open places in the towns where markets and assemblies were held. Both the town dwellers and the country farmers would share in the sorrow. "Those skilled in lamentation" would be kept very busy. These were the professional mourners, who sang and wailed at funerals, as they still do in many parts of the world where it is still the custom.

5.17. I will pass through the midst of you: In fact, of course, it was the Assyrians who were to "pass through the midst" of Israel, and Amos clearly had the Assyrians in mind (see 3.9). But he did not directly foretell their coming. Rather he saw the Lord coming, and thought of the enemy soldiers as the tool which God would use in order to punish His disobedient people.

STUDY SUGGESTIONS

WORDS

1. "Amos used the word 'live' to describe the alternative to destruction which God was still offering." (p. 56).
   What two different sorts of "life" did Amos probably mean, in using this word in 5.4 and 5.6?

CONTENT

2. (a) What is the chief theme of Chapters 5 and 6?
   (b) What do these chapters show about the chief message of Amos's preaching?
   (c) What 4 different sorts of saying are included in 5.1–17?
3. What is the chief difference between the Israelites' ideas about death, and those of Christians?
4. What did Amos mean by the following phrases:
   (a) "Seek the Lord" (5.4, 6)?
   (b) "Break out like fire" (5.6)?
   (c) "Exactions of wheat" (5.11)?
5. To what custom was Amos referring when he spoke of "lamentation" (5.1)?
6. Are the following statements true or untrue?
   (a) Amos was like the preachers condemned by Jeremiah for saying "Peace, peace".

(b) Amos was not a prudent man.
(c) Amos saw no hope at all for the nations.
(d) Amos directly foretold the coming of the Assyrians.
In each case, point to a verse in the chapters so far studied which supports your answer.

BIBLE

7. (a) In what way is Amos 5.8, 9 like Job 9.4–10?
   (b) Summarize in your own words the teaching of these two passages.
8. The following verses all refer to the same subject. What is that subject, and why did the prophets regard it as an example of injustice?
   Isa. 5.9; Amos 3.15; Amos 5.11; Hag. 1.4.

APPLICATION, OPINION, RESEARCH

9. In Israel the city gates were the place where people met for discussion, and made decisions that led to justice or injustice.
   (a) In what place do the people of your town make decisions about the affairs of the community?
   (b) How far does the Church, or do individual Christians, take part in those decisions?
10. "He who is prudent will keep silent" (Amos 5.13).
   (a) Give two examples from everyday life of times when it is right for a Christian to keep silent.
   (b) Give two examples of times when a Christian should speak what is in his mind.
11. (a) What would you do if you were applying for a job in a government office, and the staff manager said: "There are five other applicants, but I will give you the job if you promise to pay me a certain sum each week from your wages."?
   (b) What would you reply if a friend came to you and said: "My employer has accused me of stealing ten dollars from his shop. If you will swear to him that I was in your house at the time when the money was stolen, I will pay you five dollars out of my own pocket."?
12. In some countries it is the custom for professional mourners to weep and wail at the funerals of Christians, as well as those of people of other religions.
   (a) What does this custom show about people's ideas about life after death?
   (b) Do you think it is right for Christians to follow this custom? Give reasons for your answer.

2. The Judgement to Come 5.18–27

SUMMARY AND BACKGROUND

This short section contains very powerful preaching. Amos had not been trained in public speaking, nor attended sermon classes, but he knew how to speak in ways that would convince his hearers. There are several points we may notice about his use of language.

(a) He used vivid picture-language about real things, rather than generalizations (see 5.19; 6.4; 2.9).

(b) He asked questions which would make his audience think (see 3.3–8; 5.20; 6.2–3). This is a method which good teachers often use. Jesus Himself used it in order to help His hearers think out for themselves the answers to their questions (see Matt. 9.14, 15; Mark 8.36, 37; Luke 10.36).

(c) He used repetition in order to emphasize a particular point (see chapter 4, where the phrase "Yet you did not return to me" is repeated 5 times in vv. 6–11).

(d) He used sarcasm in order to prick the balloon of people's self-confidence (see 4.4–5).

(e) He used poetry, which would be easy for people to remember, e.g. 5.2; 9.1–4.

(f) He spoke of God in very personal terms. We find a very clear example of this in 5.21–23. The words recorded were spoken by Amos, but he spoke them as though he was quoting the words of God Himself. They are words which might have been spoken by a human being. But when Amos used phrases like "I will not look" and "I will not listen" and "Take away from me", he was not suggesting that God is like a human being or that He actually has eyes and ears. Amos was simply stating as plainly as he could that the sort of worship which the Israelites were offering was not acceptable to God. Human beings have to use this sort of picture-language about God, because they have no other way of describing Him. Most of the prophets and poets of Israel did so. But the reader needs to remember that there is a big difference between their human description of God and the full truth about Him who is Spirit. This is what St Paul meant in his letter to the Corinthians, when he had described the love which is God's own nature and also His gift to His people: "now we see in a mirror dimly, but then face to face. Now I know in part; then I shall understand fully" (1 Cor. 13.12).

INTERPRETATION AND NOTES

5.18–20. You who desire the day of the Lord: Many Israelites expected that God would come to judge the world. The phrase "the day of the Lord" means this time of judgement. In the Bible it is used for the first time here in the Book of Amos, and from the way Amos used it we may suppose that the phrase had come into common use during his generation. Most of the people thought of this "day" as a day of triumph, when Israel would be exalted and her enemies would be scattered by the power of God. But Amos did not share that hope. He knew that this "day of the Lord" would be a day of "darkness, and not light" for the Israelites who had rejected the truth. It would not be a time of victory for Israel over her enemies, but a time of victory for God over Israel. So Amos warned his hearers of the surprise and pain which they would experience.

There are two aspects of this teaching which we should follow further:

1. The phrase "the day of the Lord" became a popular one in Israel and was used by many of the prophets after Amos. Isaiah said that "the day of the Lord is near (Isa. 13.6), and that "the day of the Lord comes ... with wrath" (Isa. 13.9). Jeremiah said that "the day of the Lord of hosts will be a day of vengeance" (Jer. 46.10). Ezekiel said, "For the day is near, the day of the Lord is near: it will be a day of clouds, a time of doom for the nations" (Ezek. 30.3). And we find Malachi, one of the latest of the prophets, saying, "Behold, I will send you Elijah the prophet before the great and terrible day of the Lord comes" (Mal. 4.5). It is not surprising, therefore, to find the phrase in the New Testament also, as part of the special language of the Christian Church. In 1 Thessalonians 5.2 and 2 Peter 3.10 the same words are used, "The day of the Lord will come like a thief in the night". Although the phrase itself is not used in the Gospels, it is clear that Jesus Himself was thinking of a sudden coming of judgement when he spoke of "the days of the Son of man" (Luke 17.22–37).

2. We learn also from this passage that any coming of God means a judgement. Amos denied that Israel would escape while her enemies were destroyed. God was judging all the nations, Israel among them. Doubtless many people expected that the coming of the Messiah would bring victory for Israel, but that event, also, brought judgement. Jesus did not come into the world to judge. But His presence on earth was itself a judgement which showed the difference between those who received Him and those who did not. "And this is the judgement, that the light has come into the world, and men loved darkness rather than light, because their deeds were evil" (John 3.19). God's spiritual presence with His people, the Church, also means that Christians are judged according to their response to Him. "For the time has come for judgement to begin with the household of God" (1 Pet. 4.17).

5.21–24. I hate ... your feasts: This passage contains very strong

"I take no delight in your solemn assemblies. Even though you offer me your burnt offerings . . . I will not accept them" (Amos 5.21, 22).

Milk and coconuts are laid every day at the feet of a gigantic image of the Hindu god Gomteshwar in South India. At Guildford in England a new cathedral has lately been built.

In what ways, if any, can these "offerings" be regarded as the offering of people's lives to God?

words about the ways in which the Israelites were accustomed to worship. Although the people who heard Amos preach do not seem to have been converted by his words, no Christian who reads thoughtfully can fail to be stirred by this section. Amos declared that God rejected the "feasts", the "solemn assemblies", the "offerings", and the music associated with worship at the holy places. What He really desired was that the Israelites should show "justice" and "righteousness" in their personal and national life.

The "offerings" mentioned by Amos were not new customs introduced by the Israelites of his time. They were part of the old tradition which we find recorded in the Pentateuch. The special times for making a burnt offering are listed in Exodus 29.38–42; the rules for making cereal offerings are set down in Leviticus 2; and the rules about peace offering in Leviticus 3. It seems probable, therefore, that these practices had started as a way in which people could show their gratitude and obedience to God, and their dependence on Him. But by the time of Amos, the system of sacrifices had become worthless, and no longer helped the people to do the will of God. What had gone wrong?

(a) People had begun to worship idols, "your images" (Amos 5.26), at the holy places, instead of worshipping God Himself.

(b) People were behaving at the holy places in ways which showed that they thought their own pleasure more important than pleasing God (2.8).

(c) People were making offerings simply as a show, and not out of a love of God (4.5).

(d) The offerings which people made at the holy places did not represent an offering of their lives. They had nothing to do with the ways in which people actually lived (5.23, 24).

From the time of Amos onwards, other prophets spoke about the danger of this kind of false religion: "What to me is the multitude of your sacrifices? says the Lord" (Isa. 1.11); "What does the Lord require of you but to do justice, and to love kindness, and to walk humbly with your God" (Mic. 6.8). Jesus also pointed out the risk of trusting to religious regulations "You tithe mint and dill and cummin," (these are garden herbs; a tenth of the crop would be a very small amount "and have neglected the weightier matters of the law, justice and mercy and faith" (Matt. 23.23).

5.25–27. Did you bring me sacrifices?: Amos seems to have believed that the Israelites had not made sacrifices during the period of the Exodus, but had only started them when they settled down in Canaan. Thus the answer to his question (v. 25) would be "no". Amos was suggesting that at that time the Israelites had truly worshipped God, without the pagan customs which they practised later.

5.26, 27. Sakkuth and **Kaiwan** were the names of Assyrian gods.

These verses are difficult to interpret, but Amos was probably saying, "The day is coming when you will pick up these idols which you praise, and carry them with you into exile in Assyria." Some scholars think that these two verses are not by Amos, but by a later writer for whom the exile was a historical event.

As we read this passage we may find ourselves thinking about our own Christian worship and about the ceremonies in our own "holy places". If the Israelites' worship could become hateful to God, can we be sure that our own public and private worship is always pleasing to Him? Can we be sure that the rites and ceremonies of a Christian Church have spiritual value? Christians of different Church traditions have tried to answer these questions in different ways.

There are some Churches today which follow a tradition of worship which discourages all ceremony. Moravians, Quakers, and many of the Calvinist Churches have answered these questions in that way. They believe that outward ceremony is dangerous, because it can distract people's attention from God himself and can prevent them from worshipping Him with their whole hearts. So worship in these Churches is very simple, and their church buildings are plain.

Other Churches, such as the Orthodox, Roman Catholic, and Anglican, have tended to encourage ceremonies which have a long history behind them. Because human beings are physical as well as spiritual, these Churches believe that people need physical reminders that will lead them towards God. So they have highly decorated buildings, elaborate robes, processions, and all the beauty that artists can bring to the worship of God. (See also Theme Discussion on Priest and Prophet, pp. 87–92.)

But all Christians face the same danger, that of giving more importance to outwardly "religious" practices and ceremonies than to inward prayer and a life of obedience to God's will. This is so, whatever sort of building we worship in, or whatever kind of Church service we offer. Christians of most Churches would agree about the best ways to avoid this danger:

(a) Amos reminds us of the need for *humility* in worship. Christians come together in Church to praise Him "who forms the mountains and creates the wind, and declares to man what is his thought" (Amos 4.13). If we think of God in this way, we shall find it easier not to think too highly of ourselves, or of our prayers and our offerings. Instead, we shall think highly of what God offers to us in our worship and in our whole lives. It is the Word of God which we come to hear read or spoken which is great, rather than the reader or the preacher.

(b) The closer our worship is linked with the rest of our life, the more helpful it is likely to be. If we think of worship as something we do on holy days and in holy places only, then it will have no effect on our home life and business life, or education, or politics.

Family worship in the home, and our private prayers, are just as important as public worship in the "holy place", that is to say the church building.

(c) We may avoid the danger if we think of our whole lives as a kind of worship. The way in which we live will show what sort of attitude we have towards God and what kind of response we make to His care and love for us.

(d) All Christians worship God "in the name of Jesus Christ". In our acts of worship, as in our whole lives, Jesus is the Way which we try to follow. It is through Him that we approach the Father, just as a petitioner in a law court might approach the Judge through a lawyer or advocate. This means that we pray to God, and praise God, in the spirit of Jesus, and according to the teaching which He has given us. We receive God's word and God's forgiveness through Jesus, through all that we know of His love. For this reason the more we study the Gospels, and the more we try to live according to the teaching of Jesus, the closer our worship will be to what God desires.

STUDY SUGGESTIONS

WORDS

1. The word "day" is used in Amos 5.8; 5.18; and 5.20.
   (a) What is its meaning in 5.18?
   (b) In which of the other two verses does it have a different meaning?
   (c) What is that different meaning?

CONTENT

2. Most of the Israelites thought that the day of God's coming in judgement would be a day of triumph for them. Why did Amos not share this hope?
3. List 6 methods by which Amos made his preaching forceful and convincing.
4. (a) What were the "offerings" which God would not accept, according to Amos?
   (b) For what reasons did God reject these offerings?
   (c) What did He require of the Israelites instead?
5. What do we learn from 3.12 and 5.19 about the vegetation and climate of Israel at the time of Amos?

BIBLE

6. (a) Read Matt. 9.14, 15 and Mark 8.36, 37.
   (i) In what way is the language and method of teaching used by Amos in 5.20 similar to the language and method of Jesus as shown in these verses?
   (ii) Why did Jesus and Amos use this sort of language?
   (b) Read Gen. 3.8, 9 and Lev. 26.27–31.
   (i) In what way is the language of these two passages similar to the language used by Amos in 5.21–23?
   (ii) Why did Amos and the writers of Genesis and Leviticus use this sort of language?
7. (i) Which one of the following passages contains the same teaching about religious practices as Amos 5.22?
   (ii) What teaching about religious practices do the other two passages contain?
   (a) Eccles. 5.1 (b) Jer. 6.20 (c) Amos 5.23, 24
8. Amos spoke strong words to the Israelites about the dangers of false religion. Paul warned the Corinthians of a special danger about Holy Communion (1 Cor. 11.27). What is that danger? How can Christians avoid it?

APPLICATION, OPINION, RESEARCH

9. Find out as much as you can about the worship services and ceremonies of other Churches and denominations than your own. How far do you think these various services and ceremonies help people to worship God "in spirit and in truth"? How far do they make true worship more difficult?
10. (a) In what ways can a pastor help the members of his congregation to link their worship more closely with their everyday lives in town or village?
    (b) In what ways can an individual Christian try to make his public and private prayers more pleasing to God?

3. Punishment and Ruin 6.1–14

SUMMARY AND BACKGROUND

In this section the editors have gathered together some sayings of Amos about the punishment which was to come on Israel. They contain vivid pictures of defeat and sorrow. Amos had no doubt at all that the punishment would come. His only doubt was whether any of the Israelites would be saved. It may be, he said, that a remnant will be spared (5.15). But in 6.9 the clear message is "they shall die." Amos saw that the life of Israel was so evil, so far from the will of God, that punishment was inevitable.

INTERPRETATION AND NOTES

6.1–3. Notable men: These verses contain a strong attack on the false confidence of the powerful leaders of Israel, who sat "at ease" in their homes and felt "secure", expecting the common people of "the house of Israel" to come to them for help or advice, or favours. Amos used sarcastic language against the pride of those notable men who thought they belonged to the most important nation.

Verse 2 is rather difficult to interpret. It seems likely that the pronouns in the last part of the verse have become reversed, and that we should change them so as to read, "Is your territory greater than their territory?" The answer then is, No; Israel is not bigger or stronger than the other places mentioned.

6.2. Calneh and **Hamath the great** were both towns in Syria, and were defeated later on by the Assyrians. **Gath of the Philistines** was captured by Judah under King Uzziah during the period of Amos. Thus the prophet was showing the leaders of Israel how foolish they were to feel secure, when greater towns than theirs had fallen or were about to fall.

6.3. The seat of violence means the source of violence, i.e. the future invaders of Israel.

6.4–8. This is another attack on the wealth and luxury of rich people in Israel who did nothing but enjoy themselves. The picture-language here is so vivid that Amos must himself have watched some of the feasts which he describes.

6.4. Beds of ivory: It was the custom for rich people to have their homes and furniture decorated or inlaid with ivory.

6.6. The midst of the stall: Amos was talking about very young calves that had not yet been put out to graze in the fields.

Wine in bowls: This phrase shows that wine was drunk in large quantities, not in ordinary small cups.

6.6. The ruin of Joseph, 6.8. The pride of Jacob: See notes on 3.13 and 5.6.

Amos pointed to three chief faults of the rich people whom he was accusing:

1. They gave themselves up to useless luxury, and to an easy and lazy way of life that had no constructive purpose (vv. 5 and 7);
2. They forgot that their wealth was gained only by oppressing the poor; and
3. They were too selfish to care about the disordered state of their precious land and God's chosen people. This is what Amos meant by the "ruin of Joseph" (v. 6).

Some readers may ask whether luxury is always wrong. Is it wrong for us to enjoy ourselves at a good feast? Must we reject the tender meat of lambs from the flock (5.4), and eat only poor quality rice or tough old beef?

In many parts of the world today governments are trying to put an end to poverty. But in most countries the only alternative to poverty is not luxury, but an income just sufficient to provide the necessities of life. There are several reasons for this; for example:

(a) Where populations are increasing (as they are in many areas), more food and more services such as education are needed all the time. Unless the total amount of goods and services is growing faster than the number of people, it is not possible for each person's share of wealth to become much greater.

(b) Every nation needs to trade with other countries, and in order to do so its goods must sell at reasonable prices. But if all its people are to have bigger incomes and higher wages, the cost of producing goods will go up, and so will the prices at which they sell. As a result, goods may become so expensive that unskilled workers cannot afford even the necessities of life. This is already beginning to happen in the U.S.A.

The problem which most modern governments have to solve is not how to enable everyone to have luxury, but how to prevent a few people from having too much while millions of others have too little.

This is just what Amos was speaking about. He could not approve of great luxury in a country where many people were living in poverty. No Christian can be satisfied with such a situation either. We can and should enjoy the good things which God has provided for us. But we must make sure that as many of our fellow human beings as possible have the opportunity to enjoy them also.

6.9. They shall die: Verses 9 and 10 seem to be a separate short word-picture in which Amos describes the terrible times that are to come for the Israelites. He compares them to mourners in a city that has suffered a war or a plague. The exact meaning of v. 10 is not clear in the Hebrew, but the RSV translation shows that Amos was referring to the Israelite custom by which a "kinsman" or relative of a man who had died would gather up his bones in order to burn them. Amos describes how this "mourner" calls out to someone in the house, "Is there still anyone with you?" It was customary for the bereaved to answer, "No; may the Lord bless thee." But Amos was prophesying that because of the terrible things that had happened, people would be afraid to use "the name of the Lord".

6.11. Smitten into fragments seems to be another reference to an earthquake (see 1.1 and 4.11).

Verse 12 is another separate short saying, in which Amos was describing how the proper order of society had been turned upside-

"Woe to those who are at ease ... who feel secure ... the notable men of the first of the nations ... for ... the great house shall be smitten into fragments" (Amos 6.1, 11).

Two drivers of Rolls-Royce cars wait for their millionaire masters outside a luxury hotel in New York. But over-confident drivers may crash, and the great engineering firm of Rolls-Royce itself came at last to financial ruin.

How can we prevent our possessions from becoming our hope for security?

down in Israel. In the two rhetorical questions about horses and ploughing, he was again using picture-language to describe a completely unnatural state of affairs. Translators of this verse have interpreted the Hebrew in various ways, but its meaning is clear. In Israel justice had become injustice; and to Amos this was contrary to the natural order which God intended.

Verses 13 and 14 contain a call to the people not to be too confident in themselves. Here Amos used a pun, or play on words. **Lodebar** was the name of a place in Gilead, but the word in Hebrew means "a worthless thing". **Karnaim** also may be a place name, but it can mean "the horns", a phrase often used to symbolize strength as well as safety (see note on 3.13–15, p. 39). So Amos was saying that even if Israel had captured these towns, such small victories had no lasting value. The Israelites would soon learn how foolish it was to boast of their own strength, instead of trusting in the power of God. The enemy would oppress the people from one end of Israel to the other, from the "entrance of Hamath", i.e. the boundary with the Syrian province of that name near Mount Hermon, in the north, to the Arabah valley south of the Dead Sea (see map, p. 2).

STUDY SUGGESTIONS

WORDS

1. In the RSV the same poetic word is used in Amos 6.1 and 4 (and also 5.18) to translate the prophet's declaration about the future punishment of Israel.
   (a) What is that word?
   (b) What is its meaning?
   (c) To what sort of people was it addressed?

CONTENT

2. (i) What sorts of language was Amos using in the following verses?
   (a) 6.2; (b) 6.12a; (c) 6.13
   (ii) What are the two meanings of *Lodebar* and of *Karnaim* respectively in 6.13?
3. What particular sorts of punishment did Amos foresee for the Israelites in each of the following verses?
   (a) 6.3; (b) 6.7; (c) 6.8; (d) 6.11; (e) 6.14
4. (a) To what Israelite custom was Amos referring in 6.9?
   (b) What did he mean when he prophesied that people would say "We must not mention the name of the Lord"?

5. Where were (a) Hamath, and (b) the Arabah?
6. Compare Amos 6.12 (RSV) with the translation of the same verse in the AV.
   (a) What difference is there between the two versions?
   (b) What difference, if any, does this make to the teaching contained in this verse?
   (c) Why do the two versions differ?

APPLICATION, OPINION, RESEARCH

7. Amos attacked the "notable men", i.e. the national leaders of Israel who thought themselves stronger than their enemies. Do you think that national leaders should always show confidence in the future, or should they express any doubts they may have? Give examples in support of your answer.
8. (a) It has been said that a poor man regards as luxury, conditions which a rich man regards as poverty and lack. Do you agree? If not, how would you answer the question, "What is luxury"?
   (b) "Some readers may ask whether luxury is always wrong." (p. 70). What is your opinion?
9. Today the people of Europe and North America have three times as much food per person as the people of South America, Africa, and Asia.

Read Matthew 5.38–42 and 6.25–33. Does the teaching of Jesus in these passages mean that Christians should accept it as God's will that some people should enjoy a much higher standard of living than others? If not, what does it mean?

10. Find out:
    (a) What the government in your country is doing to ensure that everyone has enough to live on, i.e. that no-one has too much while thousands have too little.
    (b) What, if anything, the Churches are doing to help the poor. What do you think individual Christians can do to help?
11. Some historians say that the Roman Empire came to an end because luxurious living weakened the character of its rulers. Hopeless poverty also can spoil people's characters. Give examples to show how great riches and great poverty both affect character.

PART IV 7.1—8.3
VISIONS AND THEIR MEANING

INTRODUCTION

This section of the book records a number of visions which Amos had. They all contain the same kind of warning as the general preaching of Amos, and their message is similar to the message in chapters 5 and 6. It also contains a short passage (7.10–17) describing an incident in Amos's own life.

The English word "vision" means "seeing", or "something which is seen". Biblical scholars use the word to mean something which is "seen" by a man in his mind or in his dreams, and which brings him some new knowledge. This experience of seeing something "in a vision" is found in many religions. Muhammad reported his visions of heaven. Some Buddhists discipline themselves in order to experience visions more often. The priests of many tribal religions claim to see the future in visions and dreams. From the earliest times people have regarded this power to see inwardly what no-one could see outwardly as a special gift from God.

In those parts of the Old Testament which describe events that occurred before the time of the prophets, we read of the visions of Abraham: "After these things the word of the Lord came to Abram in a vision" (Gen. 15.1); of Nathan: "In accordance with all these words and in accordance with all this vision, Nathan spoke to David" (2 Sam. 7.17); of Micaiah: "Therefore hear the word of the Lord: I saw the Lord sitting on his throne and all the host of heaven" (1 Kings 22.19). In Numbers 12.6–8 a very interesting contrast is shown between Moses and other holy men: "If there is a prophet among you, I the Lord make myself known to him in a vision, I speak with him in a dream. Not so with my servant Moses . . . with him I speak mouth to mouth clearly, and not in dark speech, and he beholds the form of the Lord." The writer of this passage was trying to show the great difference between Moses and the other prophets. Yet it seems probable that their visions were similar. The chief difference was that Moses saw more clearly and heard more clearly things which the other prophets saw and heard dimly.

But it certainly seems that there were two different sorts of prophetic vision or "seeing":

1. Sometimes it was entirely an inward sight, as when Ezekiel saw the valley of dry bones (Ezek. 37.1–10). That is to say, it was something which the prophet "saw" and interpreted within his own mind.

2. Sometimes it was an outward sight, as when Jeremiah saw the potter at his wheel (Jer. 18.1–6). That is to say, it was something which the prophet saw with his physical eyes. But it was illuminated in his mind by the Spirit of God in such a way that it gave him new knowledge or understanding.

These visions of Amos seem to have been of the second sort. The sight itself and the prophet's interpretation of it were both necessary parts of the "vision". Words and sights combined together to carry a single vivid message.

The Old Testament prophets lived long ago in the past. But many people today still wish for visions and "signs" by which to interpret events, and there are some who claim that God speaks to them in this way. Many of the modern religious sects, such as the Mormons and the Seventh Day Adventists, were started by people who had visions. And many men and women try to find some message about the future in their dreams, or in the dealing of a pack of cards, or in the lines on their hands. A young schoolteacher in the Pacific islands once said to a missionary, "I had a dream last night and you were in it. You were standing in the valley and the sun was shining on you, and the rest of the island was dark. And you had something big in your hands, and I was coming to get it. Then there was a storm with thunder, and I woke up. What did it mean?" It would have been easy for the missionary to suggest possible meanings, and a trained psychiatrist (or doctor who treats people's minds rather than their bodies), would certainly have had some idea of its meaning. People's dreams often reveal thoughts and ideas in their minds which have been hidden even from themselves. But the sort of "vision" described in the Bible was more than this. It was more than the dreaming or imagining of human beings. It was the action of God, putting into the mind of a man more than he could ever think of or experience for himself. We might call it a window through which a man could see and understand the will of God. Christians believe that God still makes His will known to men in this way. But such "vision" is a very rare experience.

Some scholars have pointed out that this section of the Book of Amos is written in very clear and orderly language, as though it had been carefully composed. For this reason they think that perhaps Amos actually wrote this section himself, or was closely associated with the writing of it. But we cannot be sure about this.

Scholars are also uncertain why the series of four visions is interrupted by the story about Amos and Amaziah. Three visions have been placed before that story and one comes after; yet all four seem very closely connected. Several possible reasons for this may be considered:

(a) Amos may have experienced three visions before he preached

"Thus the Lord God showed me: behold . . ." (Amos 7.1, 4, 7 and Amos 8.1). "Many people today still wish for visions and 'signs' " (p. 75).

The "prophet" and leader of an Independent Church in Rhodesia claims that he can foretell the future. But the coming of a "judgement by fire" is forecast by more scientific methods, like the Early Warning stations set up in North America to trace the possible launching of atomic weapons by an enemy nation.

In what ways, if any, does God "show" people today what the future holds for them?

at Bethel, and the fourth vision afterwards. This seems unlikely, as the editors of the book do not seem to have been very concerned to put things into their correct time order.

(b) At some stage, scribes who were making copies of the book may have made an error, and put the fourth vision in the wrong place. This is possible. There are other examples of such "secretarial" errors in the text of the Bible (e.g. in John's Gospel).

(c) An editor may have thought that the prophecy in 7.9 would be a suitable introduction to the Bethel story, because it tells how God will punish the house, or family, of Jeroboam. This explanation seems most likely to be the correct one.

1. The Locusts, the Fire, and the Plumb-line 7.1–9

INTERPRETATION AND NOTES

7.1–3. Locusts: Locusts are a sort of grasshopper. They migrate in huge swarms and destroy and devour all vegetation as they go. They are still a pest in much of north Africa and the Near East. Amos described a swarm or "plague" of locusts coming at the time of the "latter growth" of the food crop. The insects multiplied in the earlier part of the year, "the beginning of the shooting up of the latter growth". So they were just ready to swarm over the fields when the second crop was ready to be harvested. The first crop had to be paid to the king as a tax. But it was the custom for farmers to keep the second crop for themselves, so every family would suffer hunger if this second crop failed. Amos saw this plague of locusts as a clear warning that the nation would be destroyed.

7.2. Forgive, I beseech thee: These words show how Amos responded to the vision of destruction. He asked God to spare the people of Israel. This verse and 7.5 are the only verses in the book which show this side of the prophet's work. They show that he not only spoke to the people in the name of God, but also spoke to God on behalf of the people.

7.2 and 5. Jacob: see notes on 3.13 and 5.6 (pp. 39, 58).

7.3. The Lord repented: At the end of the vision, God accepted Amos's plea, and promised to hold back the destruction of the people. The word "repented" may confuse us, unless we note that there is a difference between the meaning of this word when it is applied to human beings, and its meaning when it is applied to God.

1. When the word "repent" is applied to human beings, it means that they "turn aside" from the evil that they have done, because

they are sorry. We might say that they "change direction" in order to make a new start in life.

2. When the word "repent" is applied to God it clearly cannot mean that. God does no evil and has no need to repent in that sense. Yet writers in the Bible, from the time of the Pentateuch onwards, did use the word to describe God's actions, e.g. "And the Lord repented of the evil which he thought to do to his people" (Exod. 32.14). There is a close parallel to this in 2 Samuel 24.16. In both these passages the word "repent" means to "turn aside" from punishing the Israelites for their unfaithfulness. In each case God holds back a punishment which men deserve.

When we apply this second meaning, here in 7.3 and again in v. 6, it is helpful to remember the repeated phrase in chapters 1 and 2: "For three transgressions ... and for four, I will not revoke the punishment". God was not warning the people of punishment for one single sin, but for their continual or repeated sins. It seems likely that this is why there is a difference between the first two visions and the last two. In the first two God responded to the pleading of Amos; He did "revoke the punishment". But the Israelites continued in their disobedience, and the third and fourth visions showed the prophet that the destruction of the nation was inescapable.

7.4–6. A judgement by fire: This vision also may have arisen out of a physical event, perhaps a summer drought which resulted in famine and suffering. But the words of v. 4 suggest something more terrible than this. The basis of the vision was a drought, like that described in Amos 4.7–8, which dried up the wells and the natural springs for a time. But Amos saw it as an event which would destroy the whole nation. "The great deep" meant the water which lies under the earth, which the Israelites thought of as a great sea. If that "great deep" dried up, crops would fail, vegetation would die off, there might be bad fires, and the people would starve to death. We may think of droughts in our own time which have led to famine and starvation, such as that in Bihar, India. We cannot say that all such famines are "sent" by God to punish the people who suffer from them. But we can say that famines do sometimes result from the failure of mankind as a whole to care responsibly for the earth which God has given.

We may note here how frequently Amos used the idea of fire, and other ideas associated with fire. We find the word "fire" in Amos 1.4; 1.7; 1.10; 1.12; 1.14; 2.2; 2.5; 5.6; 7.4. "Drought" is mentioned in 4.7–8; 9.13, "burning" in 4.11 and 6.10, and "great heat" in 9.5. Amos probably thought about fire and heat in two chief ways:

1. As a countryman from Judah he must have been very much aware of the dangers of drought, and the need for water. Tekoa was a barren place even after rain, as it was limestone country where the

rocks were porous and water very quickly soaked into the earth. Probably in his experience as a shepherd Amos had often had to take his sheep or goats a long way in order to find water. He had lived out of doors in the heat of the sun, and to him great heat appeared to be an enemy of life.

2. Until quite recently the working and even the smelting of metals, for weapons and tools and ornaments, was carried out by local craftsmen. The very hot fire of the furnaces which were used to purify and shape the metal was a familiar sight to many people. Fire was also used as it is today to cleanse a place of rubbish. The idea of fire was often used by writers of the Old Testament in order to describe the purifying power of God, and the way in which people's lives were shaped by His holy judgement. This sort of picture-language was used to describe Moses' experience of God's power at Sinai: "And Mount Sinai was wrapped in smoke, because the Lord descended upon it in fire" (Exod. 19.18). We find it also in the stories of Elijah, e.g. 2 Kings 1.10: "The fire came down from heaven, and consumed him and his fifty". The prophets developed the idea further and used it to describe the disasters and defeats which the nations would suffer as a result of God's judgement (see Isa. 10.16, 17; Jer. 48.45); Later still, in the sort of writing called "apocalyptic", the idea of fire was used to describe any testing of the true quality of a man (see Dan. 3.19–25). So Amos was not alone in using the word "fire" in this special way.

7.7–9. The plumb-line: In this vision Amos saw a very ordinary thing, a common tool used by builders. A plumb-line is simply a piece of string with a weight fixed at the bottom. By holding it beside a wall the builder can see if the wall is straight, since a plumb-line always hangs vertically, i.e. straight up and down.

The meaning of this vision was quite clear to Amos. The Israelites would be tested, just as a newly-built wall is tested with a plumb-line. The test would show that their life was crooked, and the nation would fall just as a crooked wall falls. The phrase "never again pass by them" means that God would not excuse them again, he would not overlook their sins and "repent" or turn aside their punishment.

7.9. High places ... sanctuaries: Even the holy places were to be destroyed. The phrase "high places" shows us that it was customary in Israel for altars and shrines to be built on the tops of hills. The custom of worshipping on a hill-top is very widely practised among people of many religions. There are many references to it in the Old Testament. In the time of Moses, the "mountain of God" (Exod. 3.1) became the central place for Israel's approach to God and God's approach to the people. But it was when the Israelites entered Canaan that the "high places" became most important, for they found that the pagan Canaanites had built all their altars on hills. So the Israelites began to consider whether they themselves should continue the custom, or should try to abolish it. This question was repeatedly mentioned in the Books of Kings. Each king was judged by the priests and people according to his policy about the "high places" (see 2 Kings 12.3). Those who allowed the "high places" to remain were accused of supporting a pagan custom. Yet when David planned the temple of Jerusalem, and Solomon built it, it was not built in a valley but on a hill. Many Christian churches also have been built on hill-tops. (We may think perhaps of the cathedrals at Kampala in Uganda, at Tananarive in Madagascar, at Lincoln in England.) Perhaps the ancient feeling still lingers on, that a hill-top is on the way to heaven, and that people are a little closer to God there.

Readers may ask what the plumb-line actually was, by which God was testing the Israelites. We might say that God was using two kinds of plumb-line to test the straightness of His people:

1. First, He was using the *Law* which He had given to the Israelites long before, to be the standard of their faith and conduct. The Law showed clearly what upright living was like.

2. Secondly, He was using the *prophets* themselves. Amos, Isaiah, and Hosea were all preaching at about this time, and they all spoke of the righteousness of God, and of the sort of life He intended His people to live. Their preaching was a standard by which the Israelites could judge their own lives.

But by both these standards Israel was like a crooked wall.

STUDY SUGGESTIONS

WORDS

1. "There were two different sorts of prophetic vision or 'seeing'." (p. 74). Which *five* of the following words are more often connected with inward seeing, and which *five* with outward seeing?
   eyesight dream illusion insight glance inspection trance introspection gaze scan
2. What does the word "repent" mean
   (a) when it is applied to human beings?
   (b) when it is applied to God?

CONTENT

3. (i) Which sort of "vision", inward or outward, was Amos describing in each of the following passages?
   (a) 2.6–8; (b) 3.9; (c) 6.11; (d) 7.7–9.
   (ii) What were the two necessary parts of a prophet's "vision"?

4. (a) What are locusts?
   (b) How did Amos interpret his vision of locusts?
5. What is the chief difference between the visions of locusts and of fire, in 7.1–3 and 4–6, on the one hand, and the vision of the plumb-line in 7.7–9 on the other?

BIBLE

6. (i) What part of a prophet's work is described in 7.2 and 7.5, but not anywhere else in the Book of Amos?
   (ii) Which of the following passages also describe that work?
   (a) Exod. 32.12–16; (b) Jer. 18.19, 20; (c) Jer. 23.16; (d) Ezek. 9.8; (e) Amos 7.14; (f) Zech. 1.1–3.
7. Read (a) Isa. 10.16–17; (b) Jer. 48.45; (c) Amos 7.4; (d) Dan. 3.19–25.
   (i) What special "picture-language" is used in all these passages?
   (ii) What is it used to describe in each case?

APPLICATION, OPINION, RESEARCH

8. "The sort of vision described in the Bible was . . . a window through which a man could see and understand the will of God." (p. 75). Do you think that people today can see the will of God, e.g. in dreams, or through taking drugs, or in any other sort of "vision"? Give your reasons.
9. Are any of the folklore stories of your country about people who saw "visions"? If so, how are these visions interpreted in the story? What is your own interpretation?
10. We have noted what Amos "saw" in a plumb-line. How might a present-day "prophet" interpret a vision of a hammer? an axe? a cloud shaped like a mushroom?

2. A Crisis in the Life of Amos 7.10–17

SUMMARY AND BACKGROUND

The prophetic books of the Bible do not contain very much information about the personal lives of the prophets. It was not the purpose of the prophets, nor of later writers who recorded their words, to tell the details of the prophets' own life-stories. But some of the books do include short passages explaining how they came to be prophets.

Probably the prophets themselves found it necessary to emphasize their calling by God, because their hearers were unwilling to accept them as prophets. (For examples see Isa. 6.1–8; Jer. 1.4–10; Ezek. 2.1–7.) Christian preachers also have had to defend themselves in

"The Lord said to me, 'Go, prophesy..." (Amos 7.15). "The prophets were thinking of the choice which the people had to make between ... destruction and ... security." (p. 86).

Here are two men whom many people have regarded as "prophets". Alan Paton in Johannesburg spoke to Asians and Europeans about their government's choice of apartheid (today such a gathering would be illegal). Bertrand Russell warned a London crowd against Britain's having nuclear weapons.

To what extent have people heeded their words, or ignored them?

this way when people would not listen to them. St Paul spoke of his calling on many occasions, as for example when he wrote: "For I would have you know, brethren, that the gospel which was preached by me is not man's gospel. For I did not receive it from man, nor was I taught it, but it came through a revelation of Jesus Christ" (Gal. 1.11–12).

In the same way, some of the prophets, and particularly Jeremiah, did describe the times of crisis in their lives. In Jeremiah 36 and 37 we read the vivid story of the prophet's imprisonment in the time of King Zedekiah.

This short passage in the Book of Amos contains factual information about his calling, and about a crisis in his life when he faced opposition from the priest of the shrine at Bethel. It is the only part of the book which records anything of the personal history of the prophet.

INTERPRETATION AND NOTES

7.10. The priest of Bethel: We do not know anything about Amaziah except what is given here, but it is clear that he held a very important position in the kingdom of Israel. Almost certainly he worked closely with the king, and took part in political affairs. For notes about Jeroboam, see p. 1.

Amos has conspired: The accusation which Amaziah made against Amos was that his preaching was directed against the king, and against the nation. (To "conspire" means to plot as a group for an illegal purpose.) Amaziah may have remembered what had happened earlier, in the time of King Jehoram. The prophet Elisha, with a group of the "sons of the prophets" (see p. 5), had taken part in the revolution which had put Jehu on the throne (2 Kings 9.1–3). Amaziah was afraid that the preaching of Amos also might lead to revolution, so he reported to the king about it. The exact words which Amaziah reported (v. 11) were not an accurate quotation from Amos' preaching. If we compare Amaziah's report in v. 11 with the actual preaching recorded in v. 9, we can see that Amaziah made it seem that Amos himself was threatening to kill the king. But this had never been part of Amos' message; he had spoken only of the coming judgement of God.

7.12–13. Go: We do not know exactly what happened when Amaziah made his report to the king. But from these two verses we may assume that Jeroboam replied, "Get rid of that man Amos; if he continues to speak against me we will punish him." Amaziah used very strong words in telling Amos to leave Israel, and it seems likely that he was speaking with the authority of the king, as well as his own authority as a priest.

7.12. Eat bread there probably means "earn your living there". Amaziah was chiefly concerned to get rid of Amos from Bethel. If Amos would go back to Judah then Amaziah had no objection to his prophesying there.

7.13. The king's sanctuary: After the death of Solomon, when the kingdom of Israel was divided, Jeroboam I had made Bethel the centre of his worship. "He placed in Bethel the priests of the high places that he had made. He went up to the altar which he had made in Bethel . . . in the month which he had devised of his own heart" (1 Kings 12.32–33). Bethel was still the place where the kings went to worship, and this was why Amaziah was so angry with Amos for saying that the worship there was false worship. Amaziah stood so close to the king that he was more concerned about the duty which he thought Amos owned to Jeroboam, than about the duty which the whole people of Israel owed to God. Amaziah could not say to Amos, "Your word is a false word because the Law is against you." So instead, he accused him of failing to respect the "king's sanctuary" (see note on 3.13–15).

7.14–17. The Lord took me. Verses 14 and 15 contain Amos's own account of his calling by God. This was his defence against Amaziah's accusation. Amos pointed out that there was no question of a conspiracy. He was working entirely on his own, and was neither a prophet by training nor a member of the group known as the "sons of the prophets" (see RSV marginal note on v. 14 and p. 5). Amos had not come to Bethel as the agent of any other person. He had become a prophet only because he felt the call of God. The priest was saying, "Go, flee"; but God had said, "Go, prophesy". The priest might be speaking with the authority of the king, but Amos spoke with the authority of God.

7.14. Sycamore trees: See p. 9.

7.16, 17. You shall die: A further message about judgement. Amos was not silenced by Amaziah. On the contrary, he warned him of the terrible punishment which the priest himself would suffer in the future. Amaziah's wife would become a common prostitute, his children would die in battle, and his land would be seized by the enemy and "parcelled out", i.e. divided up and given to others. Finally Amaziah himself would die in exile. Thus all the things that Amaziah held precious and holy would be destroyed.

We do not know whether these prophecies about Amaziah were actually fulfilled; but in the conditions of Israel after the Assyrian attack it is quite possible that they were.

3. The Summer Fruit 8.1–3

SUMMARY AND BACKGROUND

These three verses describe the fourth vision, which follows very closely the pattern of the first three visions in 7.1–9. Many scholars think that 8.1–3 should follow immediately after 7.9, and that the verses 7.10–17 were inserted at that point by a later editor of the book (see p. 10).

INTERPRETATION AND NOTES

8.1–3. A basket of summer fruit: Like the vision of the plumb-line, Amos's fourth vision was based on an everyday sight, such as he must often have seen in the market-place. Amos interpreted this vision in two ways:

1. The fruit was of a sort which ripened at the end of the harvest, the end of the summer. So Amos saw it as a sign of the end of Israel's summer, the end of her time of security.
2. He also understood it as a sort of pun, or play on words, because the Hebrew word for "summer fruit" was *qayits* (this may also be transliterated *qais* or *kayis*), which sounded very like the word for "end", *qets* (*qes* or *kes*).

8.2 The end has come . . . I will never again pass by them: These words show us that God's judgement on Israel was inevitable. In his first and second visions, Amos had pleaded for the Israelites, and God had turned aside from punishing them. But in this fourth vision the end was decided and confirmed by the Lord. The Israelites had been given a final warning, but had chosen to ignore it.

Verse 3 continues the picture of death which we saw in 5.16–17 and 6.9–10. We have already noted the reasons why the people of that time specially feared death (see p. 29).

8.3. Wailings ... dead bodies ... in every place ... cast out ... silence: These words could be used to describe some modern scenes of death. This passage could be part of a report about Vietnam, or Biafra, or Hiroshima. That is one sort of end for man. It is from that result—and every other result—of sin that Christ comes to deliver us. Christians believe that there are two ends that are possible for man: death or life. Paul put this clearly in Romans 6.21–22: "What return did you get from the things of which you are now ashamed? The end of those things is death. But now that you have been set free from sin and have become slaves of God, the return you get is sanctification and its end, eternal life." Paul was thinking chiefly of the wonderful possibility for each individual believer who would live for ever with God. The holy men whose words are recorded in the Old Testament were thinking about the people as a group. They were thinking of the choice which the people had to make, between a way of life which would cause the destruction and death of the group as a whole, and a way of life which would bring security for themselves and for future generations. "I have set before you life and death, blessing and curse; therefore choose life, that you and your descendants may live, loving the Lord your God, obeying his voice, and cleaving to him" (Deut. 30.19–20).

STUDY SUGGESTIONS

WORDS

1. What is the meaning of the word "sanctuary" as used in 7.13?
2. The meeting with Amaziah is described on p. 82 as a "crisis" in the life of Amos. Explain the meaning of the word "crisis", giving 2 examples from everyday life to illustrate your answer.

CONTENT

3. Give 3 possible reasons why the editors of the Book of Amos have placed the story of Amos and Amaziah so that it interrupts the series of visions recorded in chapter 7.
4. "Amaziah held an important position . . . in Israel." (p. 83). What evidence for this statement can we find in 7.10, 11?
5. (a) What was the difference between Amaziah's report of Amos' preaching, and the actual words of the preaching?
   (b) Why was Amaziah afraid to let Amos continue preaching at Bethel?
6. (a) What did Amos mean when he said, "I am no prophet, nor a prophet's son" (7.14)?
   (b) What punishment did Amos foretell for Amaziah?
7. (a) How did Amos interpret the vision of the summer fruit?
   (b) In what chief way is the message which Amos saw in the vision of the plumb-line like that which he saw in the vision of the summer fruit?

BIBLE

8. In what way are the following passages like Amos 7.15? Isa. 6.1–8; Jer. 1.4–10; Ezek. 2.1–7.
9. In what ways was the experience and behaviour of Jesus as described in Mark 14.53–65 (a) like, and (b) unlike the experience of Amos as described in Amos 7.10–17?

APPLICATION, OPINION, RESEARCH

10. Describe any religious groups of which you have experience which were started by people who had "visions", or in which there are priests or prophets who continue to have "visions". What is your opinion of them?
11. Amos was able to "see" God's will in everyday things like a plumb-line or a basket of fruit. In your opinion, does God show His will in this way to everyone, regardless of their religion? To all Christians? to some Christians only? to nobody?
12. "The words which Amaziah reported were not an accurate quotation." (p. 83).
    Are newspapers in your country always accurate in their reporting. Do government spokesmen always speak the truth? Do the Churches always give accurate reports about their membership and their activities? If not, in what ways and for what purposes are they inaccurate? Give examples.
13. Give 2 examples of twentieth century nations who chose a way of life which led to destruction and death?

Theme Discussion: Priest and Prophet

The clash between Amaziah and Amos is one example of the difference between people who think that the "priestly" side of religion is the most important, and those who think that the "prophetic" side is more important.

Those who are chiefly concerned about the priestly side of religion lay great emphasis on having settled places of worship, keeping regular observances, and on the offering of sacrifices, the forgiveness of sins, and the defence of all that is considered holy.

Those who are more concerned about the prophetic side of religion lay more emphasis on individual inspiration, the power of speech to turn men to God, the sense of challenge and decision, the condemnation of sin, the worship of the heart, and impatience with tradition.

THE PRIESTHOOD IN OLD TESTAMENT TIMES

We have already noted something of the background of the Old Testament prophets. The earliest mention of a priesthood in the Bible is in Exodus, when Moses established the pattern of worship for the Israelites in the desert. By means of a special ceremony Aaron and his four sons were consecrated (made holy) as guardians of the tabernacle (Exod. 28 and 29).The responsibility was to be hereditary, i.e. handed on to their descendants of the tribe of Levi (Exod. 40.14, 15).

Even before the time of Moses, the elders or leaders of the people had sometimes acted as priests by setting aside places to be holy, and by making sacrifices. "Noah built an altar" (Gen. 8.20). "Abraham went and took the ram and offered it up as a burnt offering" (Gen. 22.13). "Jacob set up a pillar in the place where he had spoken with him, a pillar of stone; and he poured out a drink offering on it, and poured oil on it" (Gen. 35.14). Thus it appears that Moses was not establishing an altogether new form of worship. Rather he was arranging a regular and permanent way in which the Israelites could approach God. The first priests were appointed as *people* through whom the Israelites could experience the holiness of God's presence, at a time when the nation was on the move and so could not establish any permanent holy *place*. The priests were to help the Israelites to keep their side of the Covenant.

It was when the temple at Jerusalem was built that the priesthood really gained power and took full control of Israelite worship. The temple gave the priests a centre for all their activities. They soon became a powerful group of men, and were able to influence the life of Israel and the policies of its rulers. This probably helped the Israelites to resist the temptations of Baal-worship in Canaan. To say, "Come to Jerusalem and take part in the true sacrifices" was one way of persuading people to avoid the "high places" and their idols. The priesthood also took a large part in maintaining and preserving the Law, and in teaching the Law. In fulfilling this task the priests were not so very different from the prophets. Both agreed that the Law was God's gift and that it must be obeyed. The priests, however, were usually more concerned with the rules for ritual and ceremonial, while the prophets were chiefly concerned with the people's behaviour, and with the moral principles on which the law was based.

It seems clear that in all this long tradition of priesthood the Israelites were receiving a gift from God. God had ordered Moses to establish a priesthood which would defend the purity of Israel's faith during the early years in Canaan. It was the duty of the priests to make regular offerings to God, and to remind the people of the holiness of God.

DANGERS AND TEMPTATIONS

Yet the priests were tempted in many ways. In Amaziah we see a priest who gave in to two different sorts of temptation:

1. He was tempted by power: he wanted to serve the king rather than to serve God;

2. He was tempted by tradition and unwillingness to change: he was so accustomed to impure worship that he would not join with Amos in cleansing Bethel. He could not hope to escape the results of God's judgement.

In the New Testament we read that the priesthood was again condemned, and for the same reasons. Jesus declared that the priests had set themselves up as barriers between men and God, rather than acting as a help for men's worship. They too loved power. They too had been so blinded by tradition and selfishness that they did not see that the temple had become "a den of robbers" instead of a "house of prayer" (see Mark 11.15–19).

The prophets also suffered temptation, and not all those who called themselves prophets were truly called by God. Some were tempted to gain popularity by prophesying "a lying vision", saying, "Sword and famine shall not come on this land" (Jer. 14.14 and 15). Some were led astray by their own weakness: "The priest and the prophet reel with strong drink ... they err in vision, they stumble in giving judgement" (Isa. 28.7). Others were tempted to "divine (i.e. predict the future) for money" (Mic. 3.11). Like the false priests, these false prophets were condemned by God: "By sword and famine those prophets shall be consumed" (Jer. 14.15).

JESUS: THE SUM OF BOTH TRADITIONS

These two sides can be seen in almost any religion and any country. And it is natural that there should sometimes be disagreement between them. There are perhaps two sorts of people—those who chiefly want to change the world by their message, and those who chiefly want to preserve the past. Christians often say that Jesus reconciled or combined the two sides of religion in Himself and was both (a) Prophet and (b) Priest.

(a) It is clear from the way in which people of His own time spoke about Jesus that they did regard Him as a prophet. At the court of Herod some people said about Jesus, "John the baptizer has been raised from the dead; that is why these powers are at work in him. But others said, It is Elijah. And others said, It is a prophet, like one of the prophets of old." (Mark 6.14–15.) When Jesus asked the disciples, "Who do men say that I am?" they answered, "John the Baptist; and others say, Elijah; and others one of the prophets." (Mark 8.27–28).)

Jesus had come out of the desert with a message to preach, as so many prophets had done. The message was accompanied with signs to confirm it. These were signs by which many of the Old Testament prophets had been distinguished, so it is not surprising that people

"In most Christian Churches there is a priestly tradition concerned with ritual and order, and a prophetic tradition concerned with preaching and individual action . . . both sides are needed in every kind of ministry." (p. 92).

A congregation in the Philippines have decorated their church with flowers for a festival day on which their clergy celebrate a solemn service. In Nigeria the Reverend Sola Adeboyejo distributes literature as a means of turning men's minds to God.

In what ways might each of these different kinds of ministry need to be "challenged and corrected by the Word of the living Christ"?

thought that Jesus was no different from those who had prophesied in earlier times.

(b) It is not so easy to see that Jesus was also a priest. He did not come from a priestly family, and He did not lead worship in the temple. He did teach about the Law, and the people noticed how different His teaching was from the lessons which they usually heard from the scribes. "He taught them as one who had authority" (Matt. 7.29).

Christians normally think of Jesus as the Priest in two ways:

1. through His praying for others, as in the so-called High Priestly prayer in John 17,

2. through His giving His own life on the cross as the sacrifice for sin.

The people of Jesus's own time could not easily see the priesthood of Jesus in either of these ways. It was only as Christians meditated on the work of Jesus that they came to understand Him as their priest. Writers in the New Testament only refer to Jesus as a priest in a very special way. The writer of the Epistle to the Hebrews took this as his chief theme. He showed to Jewish readers how Jesus was a "great high priest" (4.14), not of the Levite tradition but "after the order of Melchizedek" (7.17). The writer remembered the brief story of this man who was "king of Salem" and also "priest of God Most High" (Gen. 14.18). Melchizedek lived before the priesthood of Levi was established, and nothing is known about his family or his way of sacrifice. He appears as a lonely figure, yet he stood before Abraham with a divine authority. In the same way, Jesus came, not from any regular priesthood, to stand before the descendants of Abraham with God's authority. As a priest, Jesus "put away sin by the sacrifice of himself" (Heb. 9.26), and "always lives to make intercession" for those who come to Him (Heb. 7.25).

It is not possible to describe the whole work of Jesus by using these two names, but we can say that He completed, or *fulfilled* the Jewish ideas of both "priest" and "prophet". As priest, He fulfilled all that the Jewish sacrifices had been intended to do, by offering Himself. As prophet, He fulfilled all that the prophets had preached, for the message was Himself.

THE DUAL MINISTRY

For this reason the Christian Church had to start afresh in its understanding of ministry. It could not simply take over the Jewish ideas of priest and prophet which belonged to the age before Jesus came. So Christians began to use new words such as deacon, elder, and apostle for their leaders.

In spite of this, some differences still remain between the two sides of religious life. They seem to be part of human nature. In most Christian Churches there is both a priestly tradition concerned with ritual and order, and a prophetic tradition concerned with preaching and individual action. It is not always easy to keep the two sides in balance. Each may think that its way is the only right way, and one side may tend to dominate the other. But both sides are needed in all Churches and in every kind of ministry—in local worship, in Church Councils, in world-wide communions. Both traditions are the gift of God to His Church, but both need to be challenged and corrected over and over again by the Word of the living Christ.

STUDY SUGGESTIONS

WORDS

1. Which *four* of the following are (a) chiefly connected with the work of a prophet, which *four* are (b) chiefly connected with the work of a priest, and which *two* are (c) connected with both?
   inspiration purity ceremonial sacrifice prediction
   covenant sanctuary preaching challenge observance

CONTENT

2. (a) Who were the first regular priests of whom we read in the Bible?
   (b) Why was it necessary to establish this regular priesthood?
   (c) Read Exod. 28 and 29, and then describe briefly in your own words the ceremonies with which these priests were consecrated.
3. (a) Amaziah gave in to two sorts of temptation, what were they?
   (b) Give 2 examples of temptations which the prophets of Israel suffered.
4. (a) For what reasons did people of His own time regard Jesus as a prophet?
   (b) The prayer of Jesus recorded in John 17 is sometimes called the "High Priestly" prayer. What other action or actions of Jesus cause Christians to think of Him as a priest?

BIBLE

5. Read 1 Cor. 12.4–11. What is the chief teaching of St Paul in this passage about the relative importance of priests and prophets in the Church?

APPLICATION, OPINION, RESEARCH

6. Which tradition is stronger in your own Church, the priestly or the prophetic? Are both traditions allowed their proper place?

7. (a) In what ways is the work of a Christian minister like that of a Jewish priest in Old Testament times. In what ways is it *un*like?
   (b) Find out, if you can, about the work of a Jewish priest today. In what ways is it like and unlike the work of a Jewish priest in Old Testament times?
8. Find out all you can about the ceremonies by which ministers are ordained in the different Churches in your country. In what ways, if any, are these ceremonies like the ceremonies by which Aaron and his sons were consecrated in Israel (Exod. 28, 29)? How much emphasis do they lay on the importance of prophecy in the work of a minister?
9. Act a role-play with one or more of your friends or fellow-students, in which a modern "prophet" (perhaps a revivalist preacher) is arguing with a modern "priest" (perhaps the dean of a cathedral).

PART V 8.4—9.10
FURTHER PREACHING

INTRODUCTION

In his preaching, Amos tried to speak clearly about the kind of judgement that was coming to Israel. He was not being cruel or heartless when he warned the Israelites of these future disasters. To speak of them was part of his duty as a prophet. Nearly two hundred years after Amos another prophet, Ezekiel, said that the duty of a prophet was like that of a watchman. "If the watchman sees the sword coming and does not blow the trumpet, so that the people are not warned, and the sword comes, and takes any one of them; that man is taken away in his iniquity, but his blood I will require at the watchman's hand" (Ezek. 33.6). So we may say that Amos felt compelled to "blow the trumpet", in order to warn the Israelites of the terrible things that would happen as a result of their faithlessness. As Christians, we think and speak much about the Good News of love and forgiveness which Jesus came to bring. That is the centre of our faith. Yet even in the teaching of Jesus we hear a note of stern warning. "The sons of the kingdom" (i.e. the people of Israel) "will be thrown into the outer darkness; there men will weep and gnash their teeth" (Matt. 8.12). These are not words of cruelty, or of delight in punishment. They are words of sorrow and disappointment over Israel's continued disobedience.

1. The Sorrows of Judgement 8.4–14

SUMMARY AND BACKGROUND

The first three verses of this section follow immediately after the fourth vision, but do not seem to be connected with it. Like the warnings in Amos 2.6 and 7, this preaching was addressed to the wealthy people who were making themselves rich by cheating the poor. Verse 6 is almost a repetition of Amos 2.6, and v. 13 is similar in thought to 2.14.

INTERPRETATION AND NOTES

8.5. When will the new moon be over: The Israelites were not only joining in false worship. The wealthy merchants wanted to hurry through the religious festivals as quickly as possible so as to get back to their trading.

There was a close connection between the *new moon* and the *sabbath* in the religious life of Israel. Peoples who used a lunar calendar, like the Canaanites, kept the day of the new moon as a festival day, when no trading was allowed. In those places where the Israelites were joining in the pagan worship of the Canaanites, they saw little difference between the monthly moon-festivals and their own weekly Sabbath. By the time the Book of Chronicles was written (about 300 B.C.), the moon-festivals had been given official approval by the Israelite priests. King David told the Levites to stand in the house of the Lord "whenever burnt offerings are offered to the Lord, on sabbaths, new moons and feast days" (1 Chron. 23.31). By the time of Amos this combination of the pagan and Israelite festivals seems to have been quite usual. (See Isa. 1.13–14.)

The same sort of thing has happened at different times in history and in different parts of the world. Many peoples have regarded both the sun and the moon as "powers" to be worshipped, and hold festivals at special times to mark their movement. In many places the Christian festivals are held at about the same time; e.g. in the Roman empire the date of Christmas coincided with the festival of the winter solstice and in some countries Easter coincided with the festival of springtime, when people celebrated the end of winter. This may be regarded as part of the process by which Christianity becomes "indigenous", i.e. belonging to the country and not a foreign thing. But there is a real danger in such cases, that the Christian meaning of the festivals may be forgotten, and other meanings may take its place. Christmas may become a time for great meals and neglected worship. Sunday may become no more than a day for "recreation" in the form of sport and parties. This word "recreation" is often used to mean simply relaxation or amusement, i.e. the things we do when we are not working. But its real meaning is "creating, or being created again." Thus Sunday is a day of real "recreation" only if we are "created anew" through our relationship with God in worship and our enjoyment of the world He has created. It is important for the Church in every land to preserve and remind people of the true meaning of the Christian festivals.

8.5. That we may make the ephah small and the shekel great: Besides regarding religious festivals as an interruption of business rather than an occasion for worship, the merchants of Israel were trading dishonestly. Amos sternly accused them of using false weights and measures. The *ephah* was the measure of grain that was being sold. The *shekel* was the measure of coins that people paid. So by making the ephah smaller and the shekel larger than the proper size, the traders made the people pay more money for less grain.

8.6. Buy the needy: The merchants treated the poor people as things to be used, rather than as human beings. Those who got into debt might be bought or sold as slaves, even for as little as the price of a pair of shoes.

8.6. Refuse of the wheat means the husks and sweepings from the granary floor, spoilt and dirty grain that richer people would refuse to buy. Even this the merchants sold at a profit to those who could not afford anything better.

8.7–10. The Lord ... will never forget any of their deeds: Amos made it clear that God would not excuse or forgive the greedy merchants for what they had done.

8.8. The land would **tremble** and be **tossed about.** This seems to describe an earthquake, with the land rising and falling like the river Nile in flood (see also 1.1 and 4.11). From their study of ancient Assyrian records, scholars have found evidence that there was a big earthquake in June 763 B.C. It may have been his experience of that event which led Amos to compare the disaster which was to come to Israel with the disasters caused by an earthquake.

8.9. I will darken the earth: Some scholars believe that Amos was thinking of the dust storm that might be caused by an earthquake. Others believe that he may have meant an eclipse of the sun, which people in ancient times believed to be a sign of God's anger.

8.10. Sackcloth and **baldness** were both signs of mourning. Sackcloth was a rough cloth made of camel hair or goat hair. Baldness, or shaving one's head, was not a custom approved by the religious leaders of Israel, but it was one which the Israelites copied from surrounding nations.

Mourning for an only son: the most bitter of all sorrows, because it would mean the end of the family name. (See p. 19.)

The darkness and the earthquake which Amos foretold may remind us of the events of the Crucifixion of Jesus, as told by Matthew (Matt. 27.45 and 51). It is probable that both Amos and Matthew were using picture-language. In the time of the Israelites' punishment their whole evil way of life would be shaken to its foundations and destroyed. It would be like a city that is destroyed in an earthquake. At the time of the Crucifixion the Jews were trying to destroy the "light" which God had sent into the world. This was like an eclipse of the sun, which turns daylight into darkness.

8.11–12: In this passage Amos turned his thought from natural disasters to spiritual disaster.

8.11. A famine of bread and a thirst for water were terrible things, but the famine **of hearing the words of the Lord** would be something much worse. The people of Israel no doubt thought that the word of God was always available to them. But they were putting their

"Hear this, you who trample upon the needy . . . the days are coming when I will send a famine on the land . . . they shall run to and fro to seek the word of the Lord, and they shall not find it." (Amos 8.4, 11, 13).

Today also people are "running to and fro". A Korean farmer with his family seeks a better job in the city; youthful Americans travel to Nepal in search of a truer religion; German students hope to find a freer life in France.

What sort of "word" are they really likely to find?

trust in their holy places and priests, and in their law and tradition, instead of in God Himself. Amos saw that before long they would discover that God was not speaking to them through these things. They would go from one sanctuary to another, but they would not find the word of God anywhere. They would become a people cut off from God, in spite of all their traditions.

This picture of judgement shows how religious observance can become a dead thing if we attach too much importance to it. To hold a Church service does not in itself guarantee that we shall hear the word of the Lord. In fact, if we are not careful, the constant repetition of religious phrases can make them meaningless to our ears. We can say things so often that they become no more than a familiar noise. The Lord's Prayer, for example, can cease to be a prayer at all just because we are so familiar with it. There are places where Christians attend services so often, and listen to so many sermons, that although they hear the sound of the words, they do not understand them or remember them afterwards. If this happens, then religious practices may become a kind of screen, which keeps the light from our minds, so that we sleep. Then we soon reach the famine situation in which we cannot hear or understand God's word any more. This is not an argument in favour of not attending services. It is a reminder that we need to be open and receptive to all that God is saying to us. "He who has an ear, let him hear what the Spirit says to the churches" (Rev. 2.7). If we really want to be open to God's word we must first:

(a) believe that God does speak to us through his servants, and that His word brings life;

(b) be willing to hear an unfamiliar message even if it is disturbing or accusing;

(c) be willing to hear a familiar message and apply it to ourselves each time we hear it.

8.14. Swear by Ashimah: This verse is difficult to interpret, because the meaning of some of the Hebrew words is not known for certain. Most scholars today think that all three phrases refer to the gods of local shrines. Ashimah was a Syrian god, who seems to have been worshipped in Samaria also. Dan in the north of Israel, and Beersheba in Judah to the south, were places where pagan gods may have been worshipped at the time of Amos. Other scholars think that these names were inserted by a later editor. In either case, it is clear that Amos believed that it was useless to put one's trust in pagan gods. Anyone who did trust them would "fall and never rise again".

STUDY SUGGESTIONS

WORDS

1. Which *four* of the following words express the real meaning of the word "recreation" as explained on p. 95?
   refreshment revelry luxury renewal leisure repose
   restoration release regeneration
2. Write two sentences, using the word "refuse" (a) as a verb, (b) as a noun.

CONTENT

3. Who was it whom Amos accused of "trampling" on the needy?
4. (a) What were the chief differences between the moon-festivals and the Sabbath in Israel?
   (b) Why were the merchants impatient for the new moon to be over?
5. (a) What difference, if any, is there between vv. 2.6 and 8.6 in the book of Amos?
   (b) What was Amos describing in these two verses? Give an example from everyday life.
6. (a) What were (i) an ephah? (ii) a shekel?
   (b) Give two possible explanations of what Amos meant by "darkness" (v. 9).
7. What was the "spiritual disaster" which Amos foretold for Israel?

BIBLE

8. What natural events are described in each of the following verses?
   (a) Ps. 18.7 (b) Isa. 28.17 (c) Joel 2.31 (d) Amos 8.8 (e) Amos 8.9 (f) Matt. 27.51 (g) Mark 15.33 (h) Acts 16.26

APPLICATION, OPINION, RESEARCH

9. What are the chief festivals in your country? Are they all connected with religion? What can be done to make sure that the meaning and purpose of Christian festivals is preserved?
10. In what ways, if any, are Church people like the merchants whom Amos was accusing?
11. Do you think Church services should be made shorter? Or longer? Give reasons for your answer.
12. Sackcloth and baldness, or shaving one's head, were signs of mourning in Israel. Are any of the customary signs of mourning in your country disapproved by the Church. For what reason are they not approved? Do Christians practise them all the same? If so, why do they do so?

13. "The constant repetition of religious phrases can make them meaningless to our ears" (p. 98).
    Is this statement true in your own experience?
    What can a minister do to prevent the familiar prayers and phrases of a Church service from becoming meaningless?
    What can he do to make Sunday a day of real recreation for the members of his congregation?

2. The Lord of Men's Worship 9.1–10

SUMMARY AND BACKGROUND

Chapter 9 begins with the words *I saw,* so we know that Amos was describing a vision which he had experienced. But there are several differences between this vision and those described in chapters 7 and 8. In this vision:

(a) the sight is not described very clearly;
(b) the sight is really an introduction to the words;
(c) the sight is not of a natural event, but of the Lord Himself.

The sayings which follow emphasize the character and purpose of God. It seems likely that the editor of the book inserted the description of this vision here because he wished to conclude the sayings of Amos with passages which direct us to God rather than to the sins of Israel. This does not in any way interfere with the message that Amos was giving to his own people. To understand God's character and purpose more clearly is to understand why He would judge His people so severely.

Some scholars think that the last part of v. 8 is the beginning of an epilogue added by a later writer, since it contains a message of hope. But not all are agreed as to where the words of Amos end and this epilogue begins. In this Guide we assume that vv. 9.11–15 by themselves form the epilogue, and that it was probably added at the time of the Exile.

INTERPRETATION AND NOTES

9.1–4. I saw the Lord standing beside the altar: Amos did not say where this altar was, but we may reasonably guess that it was the one at Bethel. The altar in the holy place was where people might expect to see their Lord, for it was the place set aside for them to meet God. Isaiah "saw the Lord" in the temple (Isa. 6.1). The hope of religious men was that they might see the Lord at the holy place, as a sign of blessing to come. In this vision, however, the appearing of the Lord to Amos was not a sign of blessing, but of judgement. It was a warning that God would destroy the holy place and the worshippers.

9.1. Capitals were the tops of the pillars in the temple, **thresholds** were the large stone doorways. Amos foresaw that the whole building would collapse.

On the heads of all the people: We are reminded of the story about Samson on the temple at Gaza, "the house fell upon the lords and upon all the people that were in it" (Judg. 16.28–30). Perhaps Amos knew that old story, and saw in his mind the same kind of destruction happening at Bethel.

9.2. Not one of them shall escape: Verses 2–4 show how Amos developed the idea given in verse 1. He described how the people of Israel would flee from the judgement to come. No doubt many Israelites did run away when the Assyrian army finally attacked in 721 B.C. Some may have escaped with their lives. But no-one could escape from the judgement of the Lord, when the whole of Israel would be cut off from the blessings of the Covenant.

9.2. Sheol: In the AV this Hebrew word is usually translated as "hell". The translators of the RSV and of most other modern English versions have kept the word "Sheol", because its meaning for the Israelites was not the same as the meaning of the word "hell" for Christians. The Israelites believed that Sheol was the permanent resting place of all the dead, a region of shadows in which there would be no life, and no fellowship or knowledge of God (see also p. 29). It was sometimes called the Pit, because people thought it was situated beneath the earth. So Amos pictured the Israelites trying to escape from God's anger by digging down into Sheol, or by climbing up to the sky.

9.3. Carmel is a high mountain on the Mediterranean coast.

The serpent: Throughout history there have been legends about very large snake-like creatures living in the sea.

9.4. I will set my eyes on them for evil: This does not mean either that God actually has eyes like a human being, or that He would do something wicked. By their evil way of life the Israelites had brought evil upon themselves, so that God's judgement would be "for punishment and not for blessing". (See also 3.6.)

With all these word-pictures Amos made his meaning very clear: it was no good trying to hide from the judgement of God; not one of the Israelites would escape. This whole passage may remind us of Psalm 139.7–12. The Psalmist was singing of his trust in God: we are never out of God's hands; however far we travel and however hard our life may be, God is always there and we can always rely on Him. Amos also saw God as present everywhere. But for Israel under Judgement this would be something to fear, rather than to sing about. The Psalmist and Amos show us two aspects of the same truth: that men cannot run away from God. This is our joy only if our relationship with God is one of humility and obedience.

9.5. The Lord, God of hosts: We may compare the language and thought in verses 5 and 6 to that of Amos 4.13 and 5.8–9. As we have seen, all three passages are expressions of praise of God the Creator and His almighty power. In v. 5 we find a picture of that power as seen in earthquakes which make the land rise and fall. As in 8.8, Amos compared it to the flooding of the river Nile, which brings fertility to the whole land of Egypt when the river rises very rapidly after each year's rainy season in the mountains of Ethiopia. Today the waters are largely controlled by a system of dams, but in earlier times people believed that the sudden overflowing of the river was a direct result of God's action.

9.6. Upper chambers and **vault** are references to the Israelites' ideas about the sky. They thought of the sky as a dome or cover over the earth, with God's dwelling-place above it. Many peoples, including the Polynesians, once had similar thoughts about the structure of the universe.

Today scientists have discovered that what we see as blue sky is the space which separates the earth from the other planets and the stars. It is space which men can travel through, space which as far as we know has no boundary. But the fact that most people no longer think of God as living somewhere "above" the earth, does not change the truth about His power as Creator. We acknowledge this truth in our worship today, just as the prophets were reminding the Israelites that they should do.

9.7. Like the Ethiopians to me: Some readers may be surprised at the idea expressed in v. 7. It shows us that Amos understood the relationship between God and His people much more deeply than others of his time. No doubt many Israelites replied to his preaching by saying that because they were the chosen people of the Lord, no harm would come to them. Here Amos was showing how they were mistaken. The Ethiopians were probably the most distant people that Amos had ever heard of. Their country in east Africa was at the furthest limit of the world as it was known to the Israelites. *Caphtor* is thought to be the modern island of Crete. *Kir* was in the far north-west of Assyria, the modern Kurdistan. Amos had probably heard of these places as being the early homeland of the Philistines and the Syrians.

The words of God, "You only have I known of all the families of the earth" (3.2) show that Amos believed that Israel had a special place in the purpose of God. But 9.7 shows that he also saw that God's purpose was not limited to Israel. God's plan included the Ethiopians, although they were so distant. It included Philistines and Syrians, although they were idol-worshippers and far from the truth

"Though they dig into Sheol . . . though they climb up to heaven . . . from there I will search out and take them . . . The Lord, God of hosts . . . the Lord is his name." (Amos 9.2, 3, 5, 6)

Today men can make rockets that will send them "up to heaven" (like this one launching the three astronauts in Apollo 8 on their journey round the moon), or send their enemies down to "Sheol".

But can we escape from God's judgement more easily than the Israelites to whom Amos was preaching?

of God. This truth about God's purpose for *all* human beings was unpopular with the Israelites throughout their history. Later on, it was expressed by e.g. Deutero-Isaiah, (see Isa. 50.10), and by Jonah, who found that God pitied the foreign city of Nineveh (Jon. 4.11). Amos certainly believed that God had chosen Israel, and that He had led the nation by His special blessings during the Exodus. Because of these blessings, many Israelites thought that no other nation had any part in God's plan for the world. Amos does not seem to have given his hearers any details of God's purpose for the other nations, but he made it quite clear that God loved them no less than He loved Israel.

This lesson is one we need to remember today for several reasons:

(a) We are sometimes tempted to think of our own tribe or our own nation as being very special in the sight of God. We use this as an excuse for treating people of other nations or races as less important than ourselves, and for despising them. But *all* tribes and *all* nations are God's children, and all are equally important in His sight.

(b) When we think of the Church as being the "new Israel", we may think that it is only Christians who are "God's people". We may believe that God cares only for the Church, and not for people of other religions. But Christians do not always behave as if they were God's people, and God does not care only for those who belong to the Church. God may use others to teach Christians things which they have neglected. See also pp. 49, 50.

(c) Some of us may even think of our own Church or denomination as being nearer to God, and as knowing more of His truth, than other parts of the Church. We may think of ourselves as more likely to enter the Kingdom of Heaven than some other Christians. But this is to be like the people to whom Jesus told the parable about the Pharisee who thought himself more righteous than the tax-collector (Luke 18.9).

Note: Some scholars have interpreted verse 7 in a different way. They think that God was saying through Amos: "Because you Israelites are such great sinners I will push you far away from me, just as the Ethiopians are far away." But this interpretation does not fit very well with the last part of verse 7.

9.8b. I will not utterly destroy . . . : This suggestion that a few people will be saved out of the judgement to come on Israel reminds us of the similar message in 5.15. If this verse is *not* by Amos himself, then 5.15 is probably not by him either.

9.9. I will shake the house of Israel . . . as . . . with a sieve: Verses 9 and 10 contain a final word of judgement. The picture of Israel being tossed about "among the nations" is clearly meant to show the power of God and the weakness of Israel. But the last phrase of verse 9 about "pebbles" which are caught by the sieve is not easy to interpret. Amos may have meant the few righteous Israelites who would be the "remnant" (see p. 59). Or he may have meant the "sinners" who are mentioned in v. 10.

9.10. All the sinners ... shall die is a final warning to those who trusted in their own strength. They thought that they were safe from evil, but Amos knew that there was no foundation for their self-confidence. On the contrary, the Israelites had good reason to fear the coming judgement of God. Only twenty or thirty years after Amos spoke, King Sargon of Assyria captured Samaria and enemy invaders destroyed the rich houses and the temples. It was the end for Israel. Only the remnant, Judah, remained to keep the faith alive.

STUDY SUGGESTIONS

WORDS

1. What is the meaning of:
   (a) capitals (v.1)? (b) Sheol (v.2)? (c) Carmel (v.3)?
   (d) vault (v.6)?

CONTENT

2. In what ways is the vision described in Amos 9 different from those described in Amos 7 and 8?
3. What truths about God's judgement are contained in 9.2–4?
4. (a) Of what events in their history did Amos remind the Israelites in 9.7?
   (b) In what two ways have scholars interpreted this verse?
   (c) What does this verse teach us about God's love for His people?
5. (a) Which verse in Amos 9.2–10 seems to contradict the warning at the end of v. 1?
   (b) What reasons can we suggest for this contradiction?

BIBLE

6. V. 9.1 describes an experience in which Amos "saw" God.
   (i) Which *three* of the following verses describe a similar experience?
   (ii) What sorts of experience of God do the other verses describe?
   (a) Gen. 3.8 (b) Num. 14.14 (c) 2 Sam. 3.10 (d) Isa. 5.9 (e) Isa. 6.1 (f) Jer. 1.9 (g) Ezek. 3.23
7. What truth about God's purpose do we learn from the following passages? Isa. 50.10; Amos 9.7; Jonah 4.11.

APPLICATION, OPINION, RESEARCH

8. What would you reply to someone who said: "We need only praise God when everything is going well for us; if we do something wrong we can always hide ourselves from Him"?
9. Read again Amos 9.2–4 and also Matt. 28.20.
   If we really believe the truth contained in these passage, that God is with us always and everywhere, what difference will it make to: our worship in Church? our leisure activities? the part we take in politics? our attitude to evangelism?
10. Amos prophesied the defeat and destruction of Israel by neighbouring countries.
    (a) Find out how and when this prophecy was fulfilled.
    (b) What connection, if any, do you think the message of Amos has with the trouble between the modern state of Israel and her neighbouring countries?
11. "Some of us think of our own Church or denomination as being nearer to God, and as knowing more of His truth, than other parts of the Church." (p. 104).
    Do you think some parts of the Church know more of God's truth than others? Give reasons and examples in support of your answer.

EPILOGUE

Hope for Israel 9.11–15

SUMMARY AND BACKGROUND

As we have seen (p. 100), we cannot be sure exactly where this "epilogue", inserted by another editor, begins. We shall assume that it starts at verse 11, because the spirit and purpose of vv. 11–15 differ greatly from those of v. 10 and all that goes before. From v. 11 onwards there is no mention of judgement, but only of blessing, renewal, and restoration. This message is very different from the message contained in the rest of the Book of Amos. Moreover, the language used in these verses resembles the language used by prophets at the time of the Exile in Babylon. For these reasons, most scholars think that this epilogue was written about 550 B.C., i.e. 200 years after the time of Amos.

Some readers may say, "If these verses were written so much later, then they have no business to be in the Book of Amos, and they have no value." But if we say that, we shall be mistaken. The epilogue was included in the Book of Amos by editors who honoured the words of the prophet. Their aim was not to add something which would contradict the prophet's message. On the contrary, they wished to add something which would complete the message, and show that Amos's words had been fulfilled.

INTERPRETATION AND NOTES

Amos had taught that disobedience to the word of God would mean punishment and ruin for Israel. The punishment came. First Israel and then Judah were conquered by more powerful nations. But this did not mean that God's purpose for His people was at an end. The Israelites had failed to fulfil God's purpose, but He still had work for them to do.

There was still some hope for the future. Just before the fall of Judah the prophet Jeremiah had seen something of this hope: "So I went down to the potter's house, and there he was working at his wheel. And the vessel he was making of clay was spoiled in the potter's hand, and he reworked it into another vessel, as it seemed good to the potter to do" (Jer. 18.3–4). Amos in his preaching had used other word-pictures to describe how the vessel was spoiled in

"I will restore the fortunes of my people . . . they shall rebuild the ruined cities and inhabit them . . . I will plant them upon their land." (Amos 9. 14, 15)

In 1945 Hiroshima in Japan was totally destroyed by the first atomic bomb. Today, 25 years later, it has been rebuilt and is once again a thriving city.

What important truth about God do we learn from Amos 9. 14, 15?

the potter's hand. This epilogue expresses the hope that another vessel will be made of the clay.

We know that after the Exile Israel did still have a part in God's purpose. The preparation for the coming of the Messiah was still to be completed. It does not seem that Amos foresaw all of that preparation. He was chiefly concerned with the immediate danger to Israel. But although the message of the epilogue is very different from the message of Amos himself, it does help to complete for us this part of Israel's story. We might summarize it like this: Sin leads to sorrow and death. For the Israelites that death was exile. But out of that "death" came hope for new life.

9.11. The booth of David: A "booth" is a tent or temporary building. The word is used here to mean the "house" or family of King David, which had come to an end in Israel, and survived only in the southern Kingdom of Judah. The royal family of Judah represented the national life of the people. So the writer was saying that God would rebuild the nation that was in ruins. In v. 12 a *national* hope is expressed, that the restored Israel might have wide boundaries as in the days of David and Solomon.

9.12. The remnant of Edom means all that was left of Edom after the Babylonian wars.

All the nations is probably a reference to Moab, Ammon, and Philistia, i.e. the countries which David had added to Israel, and which therefore were "called by my name" (see also p. 25).

Note the contrast between v. 13 and the visions of Amos about drought and locusts. Here the writer describes the abundant fertility of the land which will be a sign of God's blessing.

9.13. The ploughman shall overtake the reaper and the treader of grapes him who sows: The harvest would be so great that men would still be reaping it, and still making wine, when the time came for the next ploughing and sowing to be done.

9.15. I will plant them and **they shall never again be plucked up.** These phrases liken the people of Israel to trees rooted in the soil of the promised land.

Note that the writer was expressing a *hope,* rather than a message about Israel's political future. The house of David *was* restored, but the nation suffered other disasters later on. Nevertheless this verse contains a profound truth about God's continuing care for His people even while they are being punished. We might say that it contains a "theological" hope, which we see fulfilled in the coming of Jesus. Even when it seems that life has come to a decisive end, God shows us ways in which His purpose will come alive again. St Paul was experiencing this same hope when he wrote: "What if some were unfaithful? Does their faithlessness nullify the faithfulness of God? By no means!" (Rom. 3.3, 4a.) In the time of judgement, God still keeps His promises. And for the "faithful remnant" there is always hope.

STUDY SUGGESTIONS

WORDS

1. Which *five* of the following words best describe the kind of message which is contained in Amos 9.11–15?
   confidence despondence expectation encouragement hope reassurance pessimism desperation optimism fear

CONTENT

2. (a) In what ways does the passage 9.11–15 differ from the rest of the Book of Amos?
   (b) For what reasons did the editors include this passage at the end of the book?
3. What is meant by:
   (a) The booth of David?
   (b) The remnant of Edom?
4. Describe in your own words the contrast between Amos 4.6–9 and 9.13, 14.

APPLICATION, OPINION, RESEARCH

5. "There is always hope for the 'faithful remnant' of God's people." (p. 110).
   What does this statement mean? Give examples from (a) your knowledge of the Bible, (b) your knowledge of history, and (c) life in the world today, which illustrate its truth.

STUDY SUGGESTIONS ON THE WHOLE BOOK

1. What evidence is there for saying that Amos was a true Prophet of the Lord?
2. The Book of Amos is a collection of sayings brought together with an order and a plan. After studying the whole book, do you agree with this statement? Give reasons for your answer.
3. Amos tried to uphold the covenant which the Israelites had broken. In what ways had the Israelites broken the covenant? In what ways did Amos uphold it?
4. (a) Which verses from the Book of Amos would you choose as your texts if you had to preach on the following subjects?
   (i) Judgement (ii) Justice (iii) Obedience
   (b) Write sermon outlines on the following texts:
   (i) "You only have I known . . . therefore will I punish you." (Amos 3.2)
   (ii) "Seek the Lord and live." (Amos 5.6)

Key to Study Suggestions

Introduction: the Nations

1. (a) A group of peoples or tribes belonging to a country or "state" united under one government.
   (b) A smaller group of people belonging to one family or group of families, linked by kinship and language.
   (c) A nation or tribe under a government headed by a king (or queen).
   (d) A group of nations united under a government headed by an emperor.
2. (a) See p. 1, para. 1.
   (b) (i) See p. 1, line 8.
   (ii) See p. 1, para. 3, line 1.
   (iii) See p. 1, line 7.
   (iv) See p. 1, para. 2, line 6.
   (c) (i) See p. 1, para. 2, lines 1–4.
   (ii) See p. 1, para. 2, lines 4–13.
3. (a) See map, p. 2, and p. 3, last 2 paras.
   (b) (i) See p. 3, lines 11–13.
   (ii) See p. 3, lines 23–25.
4. (a) Rich: (i), (iv). Poor: (ii), (iii), (v).
   (b) See p. 4, lines 4–6. (c) See p. 4, lines 8–10.
5. See p. 3, Other Nations and Tribes, lines 1–4.
6. (a) See p. 3, Other Nations and Tribes, lines 5–10.
   (b) See p. 1, last 2 lines.

Introduction: the Prophets

1. (a) Inspire: empower; explain: expound; proclaim: declare; examine: inspect; foretell: predict; instruct: teach.
4. See p. 5, The Work of a Prophet, para. 2.
5. (a), (b) See p. 5, The Work of a Prophet, para. 1, lines 1–4.
5. (c) See p. 7, The Importance of Amos, paras numbered (a), (b), (c), (d).
   (d) See p. 7, last para.
6. (a) The words which the prophets spoke were not their own words: they were words from God.
   (b) The prophets, and particularly Moses, "knew" God in a special way.
   (c) The Israelites believed that the prophets were able to foretell the future.
   (d) The Israelites believed that God warned them and spoke to them through the prophets.
   (e) The prophets were not afraid to warn kings and rulers, as well as the ordinary people.
   (f) The prophets felt themselves unworthy and even unwilling to speak to the people. It was God who gave them power to do so.
   (g) Not all of those who claimed to be prophets of the Lord spoke with God's authority.
7. (a) See p. 8, lines 11, 12.

Introduction: the Words of Amos

1. Iniquity, sin, offence, trespass.
2. (a) See p. 9, The Man, lines 2, 3.
   (b) See p. 9, The Man, lines 3–8.
3. (a) See p. 10, lines 4, 5.
   (b) See p. 9, last 3 lines and p. 4, line 1.
   (c) See p. 9, The Man, lines 12, 13.
   (d) See p. 10, lines 5–10.
4. See p. 10, The Book, lines 1–11. 5. See p. 11, para. numbered (f)
6. See p. 12, lines 11, 12. 7. 5.15, 9.11–15.
8. (a) God is merciful and gracious, slow to anger, steadfastly loving. He forgives

those who disobey Him, but they have to suffer the consequences of breaking His laws.
(b) He is a holy and powerful being, who is Lord of the whole earth.
(c) He is a source of strength to those who believe in Him.
(d) He is the one God.
(e) He is the Creator of the whole world.
(f) He is forgiving.
(g) He is someone who has a personal relationship with human beings.
9. See p. 12, last 2 paras.

Amos 1.3—2.3
1. See p. 16, lines 6–11.
2. (a) Consequences, reckoning, recompense, chastity, judgement.
(b) Consequences: results; reckoning: counting up or weighing; recompense: payment for; chastity: purity of thought and action; judgement: deciding about the value of something.
3. See p. 14, lines 2–14.
4. (a) (i) See p. 16, Note on 1.3.
(ii) See p. 18, Note on 1.11.
(iii) See p. 18, Note on 1.13–15, lines 1–6.
(iv) See p. 18, Note 2.1.
(b) See p. 18, lines 6–8.
5. See p. 19, lines 18, 19.
6. (a) Amos 1.4, 7, 10, 12, 14; 2.2, 5.
(b) See p. 18, lines 11–13.
7. (i) (a) Syria, (b) Moab, (c) Philistia and Phoenicia, (d) Edom.
(ii) Compare the passages in detail with (a) Amos 1.3–5; (b) Amos 2.1–3; (c) Amos 1.7, 8, 10; (d. Amos 1.12.
9. (a) See p. 19, lines 8–12.

Amos 2.4–16
1. Testimonies, ways, precepts, commandments, ordinances.
2. (a) A tree whose roots have dried up so that it will not bear fruit: meaning the complete destruction of a tribe or people because women and children as well as men are killed in war.
3. See p. 24, Note on 2.11, para 1.
4. (a) See p. 21, lines 4–10.
(b) See p. 21, lines 10, 11.
5. See p. 21, Note on 2.4, lines 3–6.
6. (a) See p. 21, Note on 2.4.
(b) and (c) See p. 21, Note on 2.4, lines 13–16.
7. (a) See p. 23, Note on 2.7, 8, lines 3–5.
(b) See p. 23, Note on 2.7, 8, lines 6–12.
(c) See Deut. 23.17.
8. (a) See p. 24, Note on 2.10, lines 7, 8, and Note on 2.11, lines 1–5.
(b) See p. 25, lines 10–13.
9. See p. 25, Note on 2.12, paras numbered 1 and 2.
10. (a) (i) Those who are responsible for justice must be fair to the poor as well as to the rich.
(ii) For oppressing the poor and taking bribes.
(b) (i) The Israelites must behave kindly towards strangers, and care for any among themselves who were in trouble.
(ii) For cruelty towards the poor and widows and orphans.
(c) (i) Creditors must not behave harshly to those in debt.
(ii) For depriving those in debt of their livelihood.
11. (i) (c), (d), (f).
(ii) (a), (b), (e).
12. (a) Because when a man and a woman marry they become one.
(b) Because a man's body is not his own to do as he likes with. It belongs to God.
(c) Because through the death of Jesus our bodies have become part of His body.
(d) Because our bodies are "temples of the Holy Spirit". We must use them only in ways which glorify God.

13. (a) See p. 25, Note on 2.12, lines 1–7.

Theme Discussion: Judgement

1. Commandments, precepts, testimonies, statutes.
2. (a) accuse, condemn, convict, testify against, reproach.
   (b) justify, acquit, excuse, reprieve, absolve, pardon.
3. (a) See p. 28, paras numbered 1 and 2.
   (b) See p. 28, para. numbered 2.
4. See p. 28, last two lines, p. 29, lines 1 and 2.
5. See p. 29, lines 7–21, and read Exod. 32.35 and Num. 16.31–35.
6. See p. 29, last para.
7. (a) See p. 30, para. 1.
   (b) See p. 30, para. 2.
8. See p. 28, paras numbered 1 and 2; p. 30, para. 2 and para. (a); p. 32, para. (c).
9. Moses: (i) those who obey will be rewarded in this life.
   (ii) those who disobey will be punished in this life.
   Jesus: (i) those who obey will have eternal life.
   (ii) those who disobey will suffer the consequences of their disobedience. But God offers them forgiveness. Through repentance, they too can have eternal life.
11. (a) See p. 29, lines 3–6.
    (b) (i) Ps. 96.10; Isa. 33.22; 1 Cor. 4.3, 4.
    (ii) Gen. 18.25; 1 Sam. 2.10; Ezek. 7.3; Heb. 10.29, 30.

Amos 3.1–15

1. See p. 36, lines 15–22.
2. (a) A salesman tries to persuade people for his own benefit. A health officer tries to persuade them for their benefit.
   (b) See p. 35, lines 12–16.
3. See p. 35, Summary.
4. (a) See p. 35, Note on 3.1.
   (b) See p. 39, para. 1.
   (c) See p. 39, Note on 3.13.
   (d) See p. 39, Note on 3.13–15.
   (e) See p. 39, Note on 3.15.
5. See p. 36, para. numbered 3.
6. (a) See p. 39, Note on 3.13–15, lines 8–13.
7. (i) Based on p. 37, Note on 3.7.
   (ii) (a) Isaiah, (b) Amos, (c) Paul.
8. See p. 37, lines 12–18.

Amos 4.1–13

1. See p. 45, Note on 4.13.
2. (a), (b), (c) See p. 41, Note on 4.13.
3. See p. 44, para. numbered 1.
4. (a) See Amos 4.6–11 and p. 44, paras numbered 1–5.
   (b) See p. 44, lines 2–4.
5. (a) (i) John the Baptist.
   (ii) Pharisees and Sadducees.
   (iii) Because they put their trust in past "religious" tradition, and were proud of their position ("We have Abraham"), instead of trying to obey God and serve their people.
   (b) (i) Jesus.
   (ii) The Scribes and the Pharisees.
   (iii) Because they made a show of their religion and tried to appear to be what they were not.
   (c) (i) Paul.
   (ii) The Galatians.
   (iii) Because they had turned away from Christ to follow false teachings.
6. (a), (b) See p. 43, Note on 4.4, 5.
7. (a) See p. 45, Note on 4.13, lines 1–3.

(b) All these passages remind us of the nature of God and of His greatness. See p. 45, Note on 4.13.

Theme Discussion: Social Justice

1. Public, popular, official, communal.
2. Equality, fairness, righteousness, love.
4. (a) See p. 48, para. numbered 1; p. 49, paras numbered 2–4.
8. (b) See pp. 50, 52, 53, paras numbered 1–5.

Amos 5.1–17

1. See p. 58, lines 3–12.
2. (a) See p. 55, lines 1–3.
   (b) See p. 55, lines 3–10.
   (c) See p. 55, last 8 lines.
3. See p. 56, para. numbered 1.
4. (a) See p. 56, Note on 5.4–7.
   (b) See p. 58, Note on 5.6.
   (c) See p. 59, lines 1–4.
5. See p. 56, Note on 5.1–3.
6. (a) Untrue, see p. 55, lines 6–8.
   True, see p. 59, Note on 5.13.
   (c) Untrue, see p. 59, Note on 5.15, para. 1.
   (d) Untrue, see p. 60, Note on 5.17.
7. (a) See p. 58, Note on 5.8.
   (b) An answer might be that God has power over the whole universe.
8. The large expensive houses of rich people: an example of injustice because the owners were living in luxury while the poorer people lived miserable lives in small houses of clay.

Amos 5.18–27

1. (a) See p. 62, Note on 5.18–20, para. 1.
   (b) Amos 5.8.
   (c) The period in each 24 hours when it is light: the opposite of "night".
2. See p. 63, lines 4–11.
3. See p. 62, paras numbered (a) to (f).
4. (a) See p. 65, lines 4–6.
   (b) See p. 65, paras numbered (a) to (d).
   (c) See p. 65, lines 6–8.
5. See p, 39, Note on 3.12. The climate was wet enough for there to be forests in which large wild animals could live.
6. (a) (i) See p. 62, para. (b), line 1.
   (ii) See p. 62, para. (b), lines 3–5.
   (b) (i) See p. 62, para. (f), lines 1–8.
   (ii) See p. 62, para. (f), lines 10–18.
7. (i) (b)
   (ii) (a) It is better to listen to the word of God than to offer sacrifices simply as a custom.
   (c) See p. 63, Note on 5.21–24, para. 1.
8. See p. 66, para. 5 to p. 67, end of para. (d).

Amos 6.1–14

1. (a) "Woe".
   (b) Suffering and sorrow.
   (c) The rich and powerful people among the Israelites.
2. (i) (a) See p. 69, Note on 6.1–3, lines 5, 6.
   (b) See p. 72, lines 1–3.
   (c) See p. 72, line 7.
   (ii) See p. 73, lines 8–11.
3. (a) See p. 69, Note on 6.3.
   (b) Exile.
   (c) Defeat by the enemy.
   (d) See p. 70, Note on 6.11.

(e) See p. 72, last 4 lines.
4. (a), (b) See p. 70, Note on 6.9.
5. (a), (b) See p. 72, lines 15–18.
6. (c) See p. 72, lines 3, 4.

Amos 7.1–9

1. Inward: dream, illusion, insight, trance, introspection.
   Outward: eyesight, glance, inspection, gaze, scan.
2. (a) See p. 77, Note on 7.3, para. numbered 1.
   (b) See p. 78, para. numbered 2.
3. (i) (a) outward, (b) outward, (c) inward, (d) inward.
   (ii) See p. 75, second para.
4. (a) See p. 77, Note on 7.1–3, lines 1–3.
   (b) See p. 77, Note on 7.1–3, lines 11, 12.
5. See p. 78, lines 16–21.
6. (i) See p. 77, Note on 7.2.
   (ii) (a), (b), (d).
7. (i) See p. 78, Note on 7.4–6, para. 2.
   (ii) See p. 79, para. numbered 2, last 7 lines.

Amos 7.10—8.3

1. See p. 84, Note on 7.13.
2. A turning point.
3. See pp. 75, 77, paras numbered (a)–(c).
4. "Priest of Bethel" shows that Amaziah was in charge of the altar where the king worshipped.
   "Sent to Jeroboam" shows that he was in close touch with the king. Amaziah's false report of Amos's words shows that he was not afraid to try to influence the king.
5. (a) See p. 83, Note on 7.10, last 5 lines.
   (b) See p. 83, Note on 7.10, para. 2, lines 4–9.
6. (a) See p. 84, Note on 7.14–7.
   (b) See p. 84, Note on 7.16, 17.
7. (a) See p. 85, Note on 8.1–3.
   (b) See p. 85, Note on 8.2., and p. 79, Note on 7.7–9.
8. See p. 81, last 4 lines; p. 83, lines 1–6.
9. (a) Some likenesses are:
   Both Jesus and Amos were accused by the chief religious leaders of their time.
   Both were accused of threatening destruction, i.e. for political reasons.
   Both were accused falsely.
   (b) Some unlikenesses are:
   Amos was accused by one man: Jesus by many.
   Amos answered his accuser: Jesus at first was silent.
   Amos was ordered to leave the kingdom: Jesus was condemned to death.

Theme Discussion: Priest and Prophet

1. (a) Inspiration, prediction, challenge, preaching.
   (b) Ceremonial, sacrifice, observance, sanctuary.
   (c) Purity, covenant.
2. (a) See p. 87, last para.
   (b) See p. 88, lines 12–16.
3. (a) See p. 88, last 4 lines.; p. 89, first 4 lines.
   (b) See p. 89, para. 3.
4. (a) See p. 89, para. numbered (a) and last para.
   (b) See p. 91, para. numbered (b) to para. 3.
5. Both are equally important because both are inspired by the same Spirit.

Amos 8.4–14

1. Refreshment, renewal, restoration, regeneration.
3. See p. 95, Note on 8.5, lines 1–4, p. 96, Note on 8.6.
4. (a) See p. 95, lines 3–15.
   (b) See p. 94, Note on 8.5, para. 1.

5. (a) 2.6: "sell the righteous".
8.6: "buy the poor".
(b) See p. 96, Note on 8.6, para. 1.
6. (a) See p. 95, Note on 8.5.
(b) See p. 96, Note on 8.9.
7. See p. 96, Note on 8.11.
8. (a) Earthquake, (b) flood, (c) eclipse, (d) flood, (e) eclipse or dust storm, (f) earthquake, (g) eclipse, (h) earthquake.
9. Based on p. 95, para. 2.

Amos 9.1–10

1. (a) See p. 101, Note on 9.1.
(b) See p. 101, Note on 9.2, para. 2.
(c) See p. 101, Note on 9.3.
(d) See p. 102, Note on 9.6.
2. See p. 100, Summary, para. 1.
3. See pp. 101, 102, Note on 9.4.
4. (a) See p. 104, lines 5, 6.
(b) See p. 102, last para.; p. 104 "Note".
(c) See p. 104, lines 8–11.
5. (a) See p. 104, Note on 9.8b.
(b) See p. 100, Summary, para. 3.
6. (i) (b), (e), (g).
(ii) Experiences in which people "heard" God: (a), (c), (d), or "felt" His "touch": (f).
7. See p. 102, Note on 9.7, para. 2., lines 3, 4.

Amos 9.11–15

1. Confidence, encouragement, hope, reassurance, optimism.
2. (a) See p. 107, lines 4–7.
(b) See p. 107, para. 2.
3. (a) See p. 109, Note on 9.11.
(b) See p. 109, Note on 9.12.
5. Based on p. 107, last para. to p. 109, para. 1, and p. 109, last para.

Index

INDEX